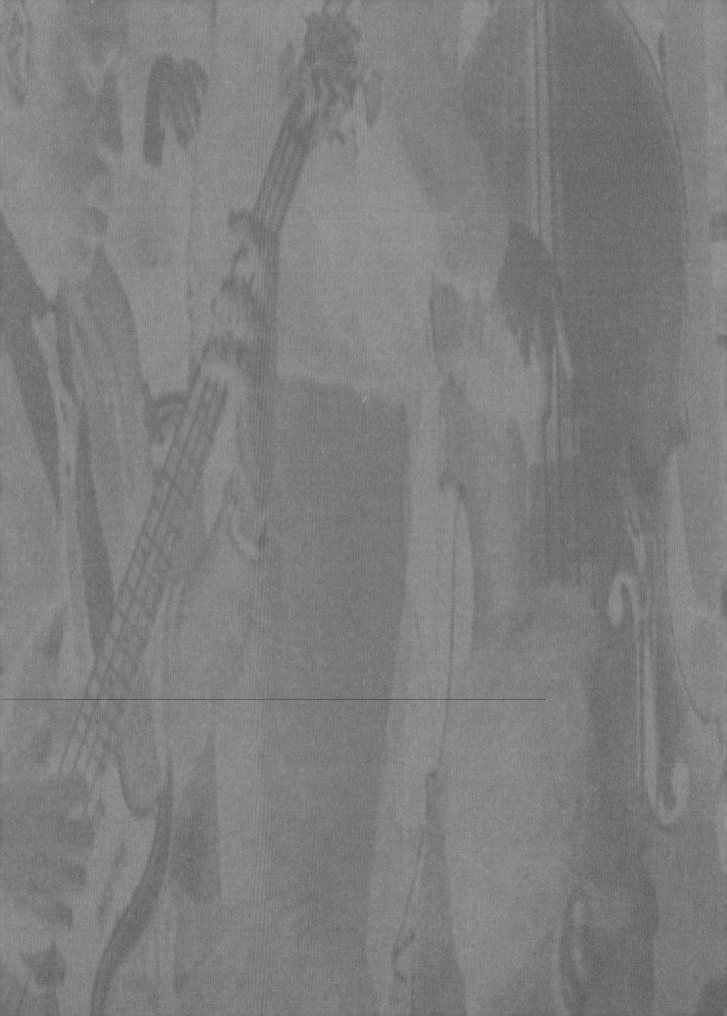

BLUES

An Illustrated History

ZEB JONES

Acknowledgments:

Courtesy of Redferns Music Picture Library: p. 12, 17, 18-19, 21, 25, 39, 41, 49, 51, 53, 55, 57, 65, 69, 75, 82, 85 and 121 (Michael Ochs Archive); p. 35, 43, 46-47, 67, 79, 81, 93, 95, 100, 109, 110, 113 and 117 (David Redfern); p. 23, 28, 63, 71 and 73 (Glen A. Baker); p. 77, 120 and 123 (Richie Aaron); p. 27, 61 and 90 (Leon Morris); p. 105, 111 and 115 (Robert Knight); p. 99 and 102-103 (Ivan Keeman); p. 88 and 91 (Geoff Dann); p. 31 and 33 (Deltahaze); p107 (Chuck Boyd); p. 119 (Ebet Roberts); p.101 (Harry Goodwin); p. 45 (Beryl Bryden); p. 97 (BD/K&K Studios); p. 9 (James Ditiger); p. 59 (G. Schlip); p. 15 (Max Jones Files); p. 64 (GEMS)

Published in 2004 by Caxton Editions

20 Bloomsbury Street

London WC1B 3JH

Designed and produced for Caxton Editions

by Open Door Limited

Langham, Rutland

Editing: Mary Morton

Colour separation: GA Graphics, Stamford, UK

Title: An Illustrated History of Blues

ISBN: 1 84067 474 1

BLUES

An Illustrated History

CONTENTS

INTRODUCTION

"It is from the blues that all that may be called American music derives it most distinctive characteristics."

(JAMES WHELDON JOHNSON, POET, 1871–1938)

The year 2003 has been officially designated the Year of the Blues by the US Senate due to the first dated notation of blues lyrics by Charles Peabody in 1903. This book is one of the many celebrations of this centennial anniversary of the blues.

The blues was born in America and resulted from a blend of African and European musical traditions. Following the American Civil War the blues emerged as a distillation of African music via the slave culture. The African slaves who were brought to work the plantations in the Americas had come from a land of many religious beliefs. These included those that are now associated with Voodoo and Santeria as well as African forms of Islam and Christianity. However, the slave masters and plantation owners ensured that these beliefs were suppressed in order to prevent any uprising. Indeed, even the teaching of the Christian religion was restricted for fear that the message of equality preached by Christ might bring about unrest and slave revolts. Instead, the slaves were kept illiterate and certainly religious congregations were not allowed. Any spreading of spiritual beliefs or cries of protest amongst slaves had to be concealed by being encoded into the call and response songs of the "field hollers". The field holler that the slaves used whilst working consisted of a calling-out of questions across the fields to other slaves who then responded with relevant information but in the form of a work song. Subjects covered usually included the oppressive work environment and the cruelty of the plantation owners. It was generally

Above: Plantation slaves in a sugar boiling house 1823.

considered to be a masculine tradition. Instruments were not allowed so improvisational techniques evolved through using boxes and the hands as drums around the camp fires.

Whereas the Northern states of the Americas had abolished slavery in the early part of the 19th century it was not abolished in the southern states until the 1860s. The 13th Amendment of the American Constitution was passed by Congress in January 1865 and ratified further in December that same year. In Section 1 it states that "Neither slavery nor involuntary servitude, except as a punishment for crime whereof the party shall have been duly convicted, shall exist within the United States, or any place subject to their jurisdiction", and Section 2 says that "Congress shall have power to enforce this article by appropriate legislation."

The musical tradition that the slaves had created was either religious or secular in nature. The former evolved into gospel music, the latter into the blues with its themes of love, sex, drink and work. This mixture of ballads, spiritual church music and rhythmic dance music, called "jump up" developed into a style of its own, with a single singer and stringed instrument and a call and response between the two.

Above: A family of plantation slaves in front of their cabin.

World War I acted as a catalyst for the blues to spread. American troops who were normally segregated were able to mix whilst overseas in Europe and so the blues was disseminated from residents of the south to residents of the north of the United States, albeit on another continent. The soldiers returned home, bringing their newfound love of the blues with them.

During the 20s the blues became a national phenomenon. Records by leading blues artists sold in millions and a new economic market for "race records" opened up. During the 30s and 40s, many black Americans moved northwards, taking their music with them where it fed into the repertoire of big band jazz. At this time the blues also became electrified and in the northern cities of Chicago and Detroit, the form of the blues band itself evolved. This was basically Mississippi Delta blues backed by bass, drums and piano. At about the same time others in Memphis were pioneering a style of guitar that combined jazz and the blues.

As big bands and jazz became the driving forces of American music, the blues moved off centre stage, until the early 1960s when a new blues phenomenon appeared. This was the era of the urban white bluesman; a time when the blues was re-imported into America via British blues bands who had been introduced to the blues through the records that their fathers had brought home from World War II and through the subsequent tours of black American blues artists. The blues now became the property of young whites, an ownership that black artists had been unable to achieve. A crossover then took place as the British blues movement toured America and then the UK playing with the top black American blues artists. As technology advanced, so the electric blues became the electronic blues of today.

This book is dedicated to the talents of the people who helped deliver the blues to the world over the past hundred years.

Above: Sheet music from the 1920s.

*Above: In Memphis during the 1930s artists were pioneering a
style of guitar music which combined jazz and the blues.*

EARLY BLUES

"White folks hear the blues come out, but they don't know how it got there."

MA RAINEY

WHAT IS THE BLUES?

The blues is a form of African-American music in which a modal melody is harmonised with Western tonal chords. The blues are not sung according to the European idea of even-tempered pitch but use bent pitches and emotionally inflected vocals. These bent pitches are known as blue notes and are one of the defining characteristics of the blues. The original West African scales had neither the third or seventh tone, nor the flat third or flat seventh and in the early bluesman's attempt to imitate these European tones the pitch was sounded approximately midway between the minor and major third, fifth or seventh, creating what became known as a blue tonality.

At a later stage, when the blues were written down as musical notation, the copyists came up with the so-called blues scale, in which the third, the seventh and sometimes the fifth scale degrees were lowered a half-step, producing a scale resembling the minor scale. Instrumental blue tonality came about through the guitarist attempting to copy the bending of notes that the singers achieved with their voices.

The lyrics associated with the blues describe desire, loneliness, tenderness, desertion, unrequited love and generally unhappy situations such as living in poverty, starvation and homelessness. The metre of the blues is usually written in iambic pentameter or AAB, that is the first line is repeated and the third line is different from the first two. The repetition of the first line gives the singer time to improvise the third line and this stems directly from the call and response field holler.

For example:

*"I woke up this morning my baby was gone
I woke up this morning my baby was gone
I feel so bad I'm all alone"*

(B B KING – "I WOKE UP THIS MORNING")

Many blues researchers have claimed that the very early blues were modelled on English ballads, using eight, ten or 16 bars. The blues now are a progression of harmonies mainly consisting of eight, 12 or 16 measures, although the 12-bar blues are by far the most well-known and are also the basis of rock 'n' roll.

The 12-bar blues harmonic progression consists of four bars of tonic, two bars of sub-dominant, two of tonic, two of dominant and again two of tonic. Jazz and rock 'n' roll instrumentalists frequently use the 12-bar blues chord progression as a basis for extended improvisations.

The blues itself emerged as a distinct type of music in the late 1800s. Spirituals, work songs, seculars, field hollers and "arhoolies" all influenced the early blues. The thematic material of the songs was originally taken from folk stories and tales of personal experiences on the plantations and in prisons. The emergence of the blues coincided with the worsening of the social and economic conditions of the black Americans in the south. The blues also follows the West African oral tradition of the Griots who were considered to be the librarians of their tribe. They kept the history and the culture of their tribe and the songs which held this information were passed on to their descendants in the same way that the Bards of the Celtic tradition were believed to have passed their songs and poetry down. The early blues singers were cultural descendants of the Griots.

Above: Slaves on a plantation in the south.

The second influence on the blues, the spirituals, were the songs of an unhappy and oppressed people. They tell of death and suffering and the longing for a better world. This was a way in which the slaves could express their discontent and maintain hope in the face of suffering. Biblical characters and motifs were used in the spirituals and the songs spoke of their eventual triumph, redemption and freedom from oppression. These spirituals are certainly one of the most important components of the black American oral tradition which continues today through the emergence of gospel music.

Above: The songs of oppressed and unhappy people influenced the blues.

The seculars glorified the ingenuity of the black slaves, in spite of their slavery. These songs focused on stealing food, escapes from oppressive masters, sexual exploits and status achieved through work or through the music itself. The work songs developed from the field hollers and "arhoolies" from the cotton and sugar plantations as well as prison farms. The lyrics talk about escaping. These field hollers were where the vocal techniques of the blues originated and were practised. The repetitive call and response rhythm was used to coordinate labour more efficiently.

African music was always participative. Group situations such as farming, building and religious rituals offered plenty of opportunity for making music. When the drums were banned by the slave owners, the slaves resorted to using their voices and bodies. Hand clapping and finger snapping as well as whistling, hissing and other strange oral noises all contributed to the sound. These were used in the blues and can still be heard today in rap and pop music. Voice masking, deep-chested growling and shrieking are other African vocal techniques which were also used in early blues singing (Charley Patton was renowned for this).

The feeling that we call "having the blues" is known as depression in modern society. People feel bad and want to do something about it. The traditional antidotes for these feelings have been narcotics, alcohol and music. The early black American people attributed these "spells of the blues" to sorcery of one kind or another and believed them to have been brought about by an enemy's conjuration or use of a voodoo queen or witch doctor. Witch doctors would sell lucky charms and fetishes to counteract the effects. The mojo is perhaps the most well-known of these talismans and features heavily in many blues song lyrics.

"I got a black cat bone
I got a mojo tooth
I got a John the Conqueroo
I'm going to mess with you"

(MUDDY WATERS – "HOOCHIE COOCHIE MAN")

As the blues developed it also came to used to exorcise despair. Eventually the blues became celebratory as more and more freedoms were gained and the height of its expression was in the dance halls.

W C Handy is credited as the man who single-handedly introduced this new style of music to the world. In 1909 he gave the world "Memphis Blues", the first documented blues song.

BIOGRAPHY:

W C Handy – the Father of the Blues

"I hate to see that evenin' sun go down,
I hate to see that evenin' sun go down,
'Cause my baby has left this town.

If I'm feelin' tomorrow,
just like I feel today,
If I'm feelin' tomorrow, like I feel today,
I'll pack my trunk and make
my get-away."

(W C HANDY – "ST LOUIS BLUES")

William Christopher Handy, referred to as the Father of the Blues, was born in November 1873 in Florence, Alabama. Like many black Americans, his first experience of music was in church where both his father and grandfather were Methodist Episcopal ministers.

As a teenager, he joined a local band, bought a cornet from a fellow band member and spent all his spare time practising. He was also top of his class in school and, after passing a teaching examination, took a teaching job in Birmingham, Alabama. Unfortunately, at this time, pay and conditions for African-American teachers were extremely poor and so he was forced to leave the job and seek employment in a local factory. During his spare time, he started a string quartet called the Lauzetta Quartet. Having learned about the World Fair in Chicago, the group decided to attend. When they arrived there they discovered that the fair had been postponed for a year. The quartet disbanded and Handy moved to Evansville in Indiana where his luck was to change dramatically. Handy joined a successful band and met and married Elizabeth Price.

In August 1896 he was invited to join a minstrel group called Mahara's Minstrels and he and his new wife travelled to Chicago to join them. For three years the group was to tour throughout the southern states and eventually went to Cuba. Life on the road was not an easy way to earn a living and, because they wanted to have children, the Handys returned to Florence, Alabama. Handy was offered a position at the Agricultural and Mechanical College in Normal, Alabama which was the only black college in the state of Alabama at the time. He was soon disheartened to discover that not only was American music considered inferior to European classical music but that he could make more money touring with the band and he rejoined Mahara's Minstrels.

In 1903 he joined a black band called the Knights of Pythias in Clarksdale, Mississippi as director and stayed with them six years. In 1909 he and the band moved to Memphis, Tennessee where he wrote an original

and the song was played on Broadway and its popularity soared. Handy continued to write and publish songs, including conventional blues songs such as "Harlem Blues" and "Beale Street Blues" as well as protest marches and fully orchestrated pieces, on a prolific scale. He started his own publishing business and worked steadily throughout the 20s and 30s.

Apart from composing he also edited and published a number of books about spirituals and the blues and his biography *Father of the Blues* was published in 1941. Unfortunately, in 1943, having spent many years with visual problems, he went blind. His first wife Elizabeth died in 1937 but at the age of 80, in 1954, he was to

song "Mister Crump" for the mayoral campaign of soon-to-be-elected Mr Crump. After the campaign he retitled the song as "Memphis Blues" and, although it sold out within a couple of days, he was misinformed and so he sold the rights to it for a mere 50 dollars. It was published in 1912. In 1914, at the age of 40, he published his most famous song, "St Louis Blues". At first it went nowhere but then he moved to New York

remarry. Sadly he suffered a stroke a year later as a result of which he was confined to a wheelchair. That same year he was given a special concert at Carnegie Hall in honour of his achievements. He was to receive many further awards throughout his life. Over 800 hundred people attended his 84th birthday party in 1957. Early in 1958 he died of pneumonia. He was buried in the Woodlawn Cemetery in New York.

Above: W C Handy — the Father of the Blues.

BLUES QUEENS

The artists known as the "classic blues singers" are all women. They had their heyday in the 1920s and the early days of blues recordings were dominated by them and in the press these women would be promoted as glamorous queens of the concert halls. They would stand on stage, dressed in spectacular costumes, make-up and accessories such as exotic bird feathers. Many of them started in the business before they had even hit their teens and were dressed to look older than their actual age. They would sing using 12-bar blues structure and country blues lyrics but combine this with vaudeville and non-blues music elements in order to encourage audience participation. As they sang, money would be thrown by the spectators and many of these classic blues women ended up relatively wealthy as they toured the vaudeville circuits.

Unlike the male bluesmen of the day, the female artists did not often write their own songs or lyrics. Instead they were given songs to perform by writers who worked for the record companies or theatres. When they entered the studio they were backed by many of the top jazz musicians of the day rather than a single instrument. Although the lyrics were in the blues style, often the music drifted into ragtime or jazz. The onset of the Depression and the rise of radio saw the classic blues decline in its popularity as other musical forms took over. However, the swing era and much of jazz owes a debt to these pioneering women.

The first vocal blues record was made on 10 August 1920 and recorded by Mamie Smith and her Jazz Hounds.

Above: Mamie Smith recorded "Crazy Blues" with her Jazz Hounds for the Okeh label in August 1920.

BIOGRAPHY:
Mamie Smith

Mamie Smith was born in May 1883 in Cincinnati, Ohio. She started her career on the vaudeville circuit, as a singer, dancer and actress. Following her appearance in Perry Bradford's *Made in Harlem* musical she became the first blues singer to record, performing "Crazy Blues" with her Jazz Hounds for the Okeh label. Bradford, a singer/songwriter and vaudeville artist in his own right, supervised the session as well as convincing the record companies that a black artist would sell. "Crazy Blues" was to pave the way for numerous female vocalists as it sold over 75,000 copies within a month of being released. It also ensured the continued interest of the record companies. Following its success, Mamie Smith continued to record. Among her accompanying musicians were Willie "The Lion" Smith and the jazz legend Coleman Hawkins. She also made three films, although by 1923 her career was effectively over.

Mamie Smith was an exuberant personality and although she had a very successful career, her love of spending and living life to the full meant that when she died in 1946 she was bankrupt.

The release of Mamie Smith's "Crazy Blues" launched a new genre in the recording industry, that of "race records" with black Americans for the first time being targeted by the record companies as potential consumers.

Although Ma Rainey was not the first blueswoman, her impact on the music was profound and she was to set many of the standards.

Above: Mamie Smith – the first voice of the blues.

BIOGRAPHY:

Ma Rainey – the Mother of the Blues

Ma Rainey was born Gertrude Pridgett in 1886 in Columbus, Georgia. In 1904 she married Will Rainey, a singer in a minstrel show. The couple toured with the Rabbitfoot Minstrels, billed as "Ma and Pa Rainey, Assassinators of the Blues". Ma is noted as the first blues singer to work in minstrel shows.

Although she had a large following throughout the south, she was unknown elsewhere until she recorded for Paramount Records in 1923, having already had a career spanning 25 years. Ma began to tour in the north where she was also billed as "Madam Rainey". During her long career she made 92 recordings for Paramount, being accompanied by such greats as Louis Armstrong and Buster Bailey. Her songs included "C C Rider" and "Jelly Bean Blues".

Ma Rainey earned huge respect from her fellow musicians and was greatly loved by her audiences for her larger-than-life but generous personality. She wore extravagant attire including a necklace made from gold coins, and was a foster-mother to some seven children. She even coached the young Bessie Smith when she joined the Rabbitfoot Minstrel show around 1914.

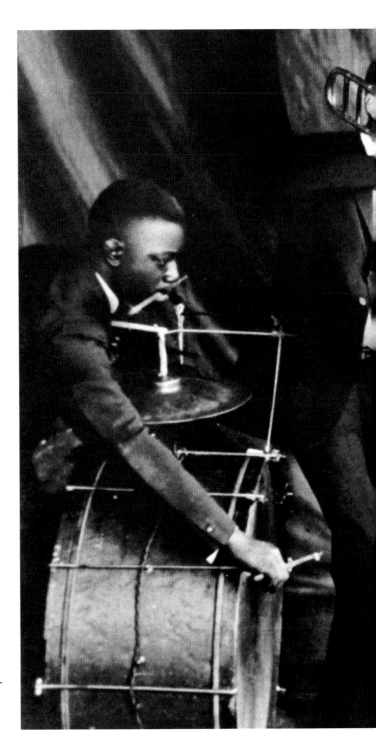

Above: Ma Rainey — the Mother of the Blues.

Bessie Smith

She also fought for women's rights and was renowned for her bisexual leanings, at one time even being arrested for hosting an indecent party at which women had been found in compromising positions.

Ma Rainey retired from music in 1935 due to waning public interest in the classic blues genre. She returned to live in her home town, earning her living through running her own theatres, as well as being active in the local Baptist church and community. She died in December 1939 from heart disease.

Bessie Smith left behind a legacy of over 160 recordings and is considered by many as the greatest blues singer of all time.

Bessie Smith was born in Chattanooga, Tennessee, in the late 1890s. She was discovered by Ma Rainey when Ma's revue passed through Chattanooga in 1912 and she heard Bessie sing. Rainey took Smith on the road with her and taught her the intricacies of the blues.

Smith's first recording, "Downhearted Blues" was released early in 1923 and was an immediate success, selling over two million copies by the end of the first year of its release. As a result of this huge hit, she began touring the best race-artist vaudeville circuits. During the mid-1920s she toured the entire south and most of the north of the United States. She was the highest-paid black entertainer of her time, earning the unprecedented amount of US$1,500 per week. She recorded with most of the top artists of the time, including Louis Armstrong, Fletcher Henderson and Sidney Bechet.

Unfortunately, during the 1930s her career began to slip into a downward spiral due to a heavy drink problem. Her business affairs had also been mismanaged. Her tribute songs to gin are well known, including "Me and My Gin", "Gin House Blues" and the prophetic "Nobody Knows You When You're Down and Out". Smith's last recording session was in 1933 and her career all but dried up; her last appearance was in New York in 1936. In September 1937 she was involved in a fatal car accident near Clarksdale, Mississippi.

"No time to marry, no time to settle down; I'm a young woman, and I ain't done runnin' around."

BESSIE SMITH –
"YOUNG WOMAN'S BLUES" (1927)

Above: Bessie Smith – the Empress of the Blues.

BIOGRAPHY:

Sippie Wallace

Beulah Thomas, later known as "Sippie", was born in 1898 in Houston, Texas. She came from a musical family and both her brothers Hersal and George went on to became famous pianists. She learned to play the piano early on and sang in her local church choir. She and her brothers would go to as many vaudeville shows as they could sneak into and by her mid-teens she had started to perform on the local circuits. In 1915 she and George moved to New Orleans and began to perform together. It was there that she worked with Louis Armstrong through her association with George. In 1917 she met and married Matt Wallace and changed her name.

In 1923, Sippie, her husband and her two brothers moved to Chicago and it was there that she cut a number of recordings, the first of which was "Up the Country Blues" on the Okeh label. Many of the great musicians of that era, such as Joe "King" Oliver, accompanied her. She was also unusual among female blues singer of the time in that she often wrote her own material. She continued to record over the next four years although the end of the 1920s saw her popularity decline. A series of tragic deaths finally took their toll on her and she retired from the music industry altogether. Firstly, in 1926, Hersal died from food poisoning and then in 1936 she lost Matt and then George (who was hit by a street car). In her grief she involved herself in her local community church, having moved to Detroit, Michigan, by this time. It was not until the folk and blues revival of the 1960s that the world was to hear from her again (apart from a short recording session in 1945) and she and fellow classic blues artist Victoria Spivey teamed up both on tours and in the studio.

In 1970, Wallace suffered a stroke which left her wheelchair-bound. Fortunately, by the 1980s she had made a recovery and in 1983 released the award-winning album *Sippie*, encouraged and accompanied by the modern blues lady Bonnie Raitt. Wallace continued to tour for the next few years and finally died on her birthday in November 1986.

Above: Sippie Wallace — Queen of the Blues.

BIOGRAPHY:

Billie Holiday

Billie Holiday was born Eleanora Fagan in Baltimore in 1915. Her parents were unmarried teenagers. Her father was a musician called Clarence Holiday; he was rarely at home and during her youth her home life was very unstable. She soon became a juvenile delinquent and from the age of 12 was also working as a prostitute.

In the late 1920s, Baltimore was hit by the Depression and so she and her mother packed their bags and went to New York. They did anything to earn a living, including prostitution. Eleanora auditioned as a dancer and then managed to get a job as a club singer. Now she changed her name to Billie Holiday, taking her father's name and that of her favourite film star Billie Dove. She very quickly earned a reputation for her powerful and earthy voice and was soon in demand in the clubs and speakeasies of New York. She was taken on by John Hammond of Columbia Records who began to manage her professional life and it was not long before she had a large fan base. In 1933 Hammond set up some recording sessions with the Benny Goodman band and this kickstarted her career.

By 1935, at the age of 20, Billie was regarded as one of the hottest jazz singers around. She began working with the best bands of the time, such as

Duke Ellington, Count Basie and Artie Shaw. Her emotive voice added a new dimension to jazz but she also sang a repertoire of blues songs. In 1938 she began singing as a solo artist and was resident at the Greenwich Village club called Café Society. Three years later she married Jimmy Munroe, who unfortunately introduced her to opiates. The marriage was short-lived, but by the end of it she was a heroin addict. By now she was earning a thousand dollars a week, which was extraordinary for the time. Sadly, most of it was spent on her "habit". She was at the peak of her career with hits such as "God Bless the Child". In 1943 she was voted as Best Jazz Vocalist in *Esquire* magazine.

The Decca recording company took her on and made a set of 36 sides now regarded as amongst the greatest jazz and blues recordings of all time. In 1945 she married trumpet player Joe Guy and fronted his band. The marriage ended two years later and Billie was arrested due to her ever-increasing drug problems. She spent a year and a day in a drug rehabilitation centre and, although she was banned from playing clubs, just ten days after her release she was playing Carnegie Hall in New York.

In 1954 Billie toured Europe. The tour included a show-stopping concert at London's Albert Hall before an audience of over 6,000. In 1956 her autobiography was published, entitled *Lady Sings the Blues*. For the first time her fans were introduced to the dark side of her life and her heroin and alcohol addictions. Unfortunately, she became more and more debilitated and her talent began to wane under the pressure. In July 1959 she was arrested for possession of heroin and died in a New York hospital.

Above: Billie Holiday – Lady Sings the Blues.

COUNTRY BLUES

"Ain't no heaven, ain't no burnin' hell,
where I'm going when I die, can't nobody tell"

SON HOUSE

MISSISSIPPI DELTA BLUES

The Mississippi Delta is an area steeped in blues legends. The homeland of the Delta blues stretches from Vicksburg, Mississippi, in the south to Memphis, Tennessee, in the north and from central Mississippi in the east to the Ozark plateau of Arkansas in the west. The Mississippi river is 2,552 miles long from its headwaters in northern Minnesota to the Gulf of Mexico in Louisiana. It is the longest river in North American and passes through ten states which are, from north to south:

Minnesota
Wisconsin
Iowa
Illinois
Missouri
Kentucky
Tennessee
Arkansas
Mississippi
Louisiana

More than 12 million people currently live in the 125 parishes and counties that border the Mississippi river.

Before 1840 the Delta was largely uninhabited. The flood plain of the Mississippi river is extremely fertile and rich and so the area is ideal for growing cotton. White plantation owners began to move into the Delta, bringing their workforce of slaves with them.

Above: The idea of personal mobility equated with freedom, the hope of better working conditions and new places is the theme of many blues songs.

After the end of the Civil War the south was forced to abandon slavery but it did not abandon the plantation economy. Black Americans still provided the main labour force but now it was through a system of sharecropping and tenant farming. However, the blacks gave up a large share of their crops to the white landowners who provided them with the use of lands, tools and clothing and, because of the corruption of many of the white landholders, the black Americans often ended up owing them more than they produced.

By the end of the 19th century and beginning of the 20th a huge black American population lived and worked in the Delta, often living in poverty with their incomes derived from sharecropping. Although they outnumbered the white population four to one, the only way for the blacks to escape this perpetual debt to white landowners was to move away. Many families moved every two or three years to escape debt. This idea of personal mobility equated with freedom, the hope of better working conditions and new places is the theme of many blues songs.

Above: After the end of the Civil War the south was forced to abandon slavery but black Americans still provided the main labour force but now it was through a system of sharecropping and tenant farming.

juke joints and at the lively dances held in work camps. It was necessary for the musicians to have great physical stamina and a broad and energetic repertoire of tunes. The musicians who could not earn a full-time living from music would supplement their incomes with odd jobs and stints at agricultural labouring. Their songs focused on the day-to-day activities of their audiences with themes such as lost love or poverty, serving as an emotional outlet for all the suffering in their lives. It was against this backdrop that the blues first emerged from the Delta – quite when is uncertain, as we have no recorded and precious little written evidence before the 1910s and 1920s.

The Delta people worked hard but expected to play hard, too, and they sought out music to act as a soundtrack to their lives. The musicians of the region made their living by acting as wandering minstrels, moving from community to community, playing in the

Delta blues is the simplest form of the blues and has very little in the way of ornamentation. The vocals are often harsh and raspy, like the original field hollers. The blues songs were mostly serious in nature, reflecting the hard lives of the musicians and their audiences. In addition to the cotton plantations, the Delta also had a large

Above: The blues songs were mostly serious in nature, reflecting the hard lives of the musicians and their audiences.

workforce for building and maintaining the levees, which were flood defences against the river. These labourers lived on the levee sites; all food, clothing and entertainment were provided by the contractor to the labourers, often at exorbitant prices – so again they often ended up owing money, rather than earning money. However, these labour contractors were among the first to hire bluesmen to play to their audience on weekends.

The first notation of Delta blues lyrics was made in 1903 by Charles Peabody, an archaeologist who listened to the songs of the black workers that he used as diggers on a site near Stobell, Mississippi. Many of the songs that he wrote down, however, were improvised on the spot. During the same year Howard Odum, a folklorist, travelled throughout the Mississippi Delta and more than half the songs he noted were blues songs. These songs had begun in the fields, but when instruments were added they were performed at recreational gatherings.

The guitar, harmonica and sometimes the piano soon began to replace the banjo and fiddle as instruments of choice among the black musicians. The tradition of Saturday night dances originated during slavery times as the slaves worked six days a week and the only time allotted for recreation was Saturday night. Many of the early bluesmen started out by playing on home-made one-stringed instruments, plucking a taut wire with a rhythmic pattern and sometimes sliding a glass bottle along the wire to control tone. This technique soon became transferred to the guitar and the bottleneck slide guitar became synonymous with early Delta blues.

Above: A blues harmonica.

BIOGRAPHY:

Charley Patton

Charley Patton was the first great Delta bluesman. Although little is known of his early life, it is believed that he was born in 1891. While he was still a child his family moved from the Mississippi hill country to the Delta in order to work on a plantation.

By 1915, he was already one of the Delta's most prominent bluesmen playing at picnics, parties, juke joints and levee camps. In addition to being a bluesman, he might also be considered the first rock 'n' roller: it was not unusual for him to play his guitar behind his knees or behind his back as well as playing loud and rough, all the while jumping around the stage. He was an inveterate showman. Patton drank and smoked excessively and purportedly had a total of eight wives. He was superstitious, arrogant and belligerent which often got him into trouble.

In 1929 he finally got a chance to record. The first song he recorded was "Pony Blues" for the Paramount label. This became his signature tune. He recorded 14 sides for Paramount which were released in 1930. In 1934 Patton travelled to New York and, despite his failing health, brought on by the excesses of his lifestyle, recorded for the American Record Company. He returned to Mississippi and a few months later died at the age of 43.

Legend has it that the bluesman Robert Johnson sold his soul to the Devil at a crossroads in return for guitar-playing talent. Certainly his talent could be deemed as supernatural but his real story is even more interesting.

Above: Charley Patton, the first great Delta bluesman.

BIOGRAPHY:
Robert Johnson

Robert Johnson was born in May 1911 in Hazlehurst, Mississippi but his family soon moved to Memphis in Tennessee. In his early teens he began playing the harmonica, which became his main instrument for the next few years. He was an underachiever at school and his bad eyesight gave him the excuse he needed to leave.

In the 1920s, Johnson took up the guitar and, having made a rack for his harmonica out of baling wire and string, he began accompanying himself. Even though he was playing a great deal of music at this time, he was reluctant to consider himself anything but a farmer. In February 1929 he married Virginia Travis. Sadly he was to lose her when she died giving birth to their first child, who was stillborn. In order to heal from this double tragedy he immersed himself in his music. He decided to leave home and began playing at the juke joints, road gangs and lumber camps.

In 1931 he was to secretly marry a woman ten years his senior, Calletta Craft. She idolised him and treated him like a king. Calletta loved to dance and she frequently went with him on gigs. Johnson was a small-boned man with long, delicate fingers, wavy hair and always appeared a lot younger than he was. He was not cut out for the physical work and hard labour that black Americans of the time were forced into.

Above: Robert Johnson.

Calletta bought him well-made clothes and he always had well-shined shoes. Despite his wife's robust figure, she was not a strong woman; her efforts to look after their family broke her health and she died after only a few years of marriage. Johnson continued to travel up and down the Mississippi river in his usual haunts and even went to New York in later years before settling down in Helena, Arkansas.

All the great musicians of the time visited and played in Helena, with its many nightclubs. Johnson played with them all and left his mark on most of them. Moving around the way he did and playing in so many places to so many different people meant that he had, out of necessity, to be able to play almost anything that was requested of him. He developed a large repertoire that included all the popular tunes of the day as well as hillbilly songs and ballads. He had the ability to listen to a song once and then play it back, note for note.

As he got older he unfortunately developed a taste for drink, gambling and drugs and would often get into fights whilst inebriated, although generally he was a sober man. He was also the subject of much adoration and attention from female fans and was never short of female company on his travels.

Johnson's first recording session was for the Vocalion label in November 1936. His second and final recording session was in June 1937. In all he recorded a total of 29 songs, 22 of which were on Vocalion, including his first bestseller, "Terraplane Blues" and subsequent songs such as "Cross Road Blues", "Love in Vain" and "Sweet Home Chicago".

He went on tour with Johnny Shines and Calvin Frasier to Chicago and St Louis, meeting and playing with many famous bluesmen of those cities. The tour went to Detroit in Michigan and then crossed the border into Canada. Before returning to Memphis he made brief stops in New York and New Jersey. However, because of his ability to play anything that an audience wanted, he focused less and less on the blues.

In 1938 Johnson left Helena in order to play a gig at a juke joint called the Three Forks in Greenwood, down in the Delta. On Saturday night 13 August 1938, Sonny Boy Williamson was the top billing at the venue and Robert Johnson played with him. This was the last time that Johnson would play the blues as he fell sick. He died on 16 August 1938; it was suggested later that he had been poisoned with whiskey laced with strychnine by a jealous husband.

One of the most amazing slide guitarists, who taught and inspired Robert Johnson and many other of the top bluesmen of the time, was Son House.

Above: Robert Johnson played with all of the great performers of his time and left his mark on most of them.

BIOGRAPHY:

Son House

Eddie James House Jr, known as Son House, was born in Riverton, Mississippi, in 1902. When he was eight his parents separated and he, his mother and brothers moved to Tallulah, Louisiana. His love of religion was immense and by the age of 15 he was already preaching sermons and was soon to become a Baptist preacher. In 1928 he took up the guitar, having been inspired by the slide guitar work of Willie Wilson who would wear a medicine bottle on his fingers to play.

He broke away from his ministry and joined Willie Brown and Charley Patton, playing at juke joints and parties in the Mississippi Delta area until 1942, when he decided to move to New York. His first recording session had been for Paramount in the 1930s and this era found him at the peak of his playing. He even taught Muddy Waters and Robert Johnson some slide techniques at this time.

He worked outside of music from 1948 to 1964, when he was "rediscovered". He played at folk and blues festivals in Washington, Philadelphia and Newport (Rhode Island). Although he had problems with alcohol, the new audiences of the 1960s so inspired him that he began to record again and he made the classic *Son House: The Legendary Father of Folk Blues* for Columbia in 1963. After the Montreux Jazz Festival he toured and recorded in England, in universities and clubs.

His health deteriorated in the early 1970s due to cancer and he was forced into retirement. He died in Detroit, Michigan in October 1988.

By the early 1920s, the terrible living and working conditions imposed on black American people in the Mississippi Delta caused the beginnings of a massive migration and at the forefront of this migration were many of Mississippi's finest blues musicians.

Above: Son House – the Father of Folk Blues.

TEXAS PRISON BLUES

"Hey mister jailer please, will you please bring me the key?

Hey mister jailer, will you please sir bring me the key?

I just want you to open the door, cause this ain't no place for me"

(LIGHTNIN' HOPKINS – JAILHOUSE BLUES)

The first area that the Delta bluesmen moved to was the cotton belt of Texas, an area rimmed by Houston, Austin and Dallas. Many former slaves had been moved into this area during the Civil War to avoid the Emancipation Proclamation which would have freed them and so there was an ideal audience already there. Texas also had a large and infamous prison farm system with gangs of prisoners, predominantly black, who were leased to white landowners; this too helped keep the work song alive in the form of chain gang songs. The vocals of this East Texas blues are much breathier and less raspy than Delta blues and feature a steady, thumping ground beat. Texas itself was rather isolated from the entertainment industry so stars and repertoires were able to mature without commercial influences.

In 1925 Blind Lemon Jefferson became the first southern self-accompanied folk blues artist to succeed commercially on records. Until then the only successful blues recording artists had been women. He was considered the greatest virtuoso Texan guitarist of the late 1920s.

Above: Blind Lemon Jefferson – King of the Country Blues.

BIOGRAPHY:
Blind Lemon Jefferson

Jefferson was born in 1897 in Wortham, Texas. Although he was blind from birth he was determined not to let his disability curtail his spirit for adventure. In his early teens he went out with his guitar as a wandering minstrel to the large towns and cities of Texas such as Dallas and played at parties and picnics. It was an unstable kind of existence and in addition to singing, he exploited his enormous size and strength by earning money through working as a wrestler.

Jefferson had a strong, clear voice and a gift for writing lyrics. He was a true innovator when it came to the technical aspects of guitar playing. The Texas style of folk blues guitar incorporated rhythmic thumping on the bass string whilst playing a rhythmically regular figure on the treble strings. The vocal line would then be followed by improvised guitar work. Many of the Mississippi bluesmen accused Jefferson of not playing in time and performing music that was not danceable. Nevertheless his popularity soared and indeed many other artists tried to emulate his sound, although this was mostly unsuccessful.

In 1925, while Jefferson was playing on the streets of Dallas, an owner of a local music shop saw him and paid for him to go to Chicago to make a record.

His first record and all that followed were instant hits. His lyrics often contained images of sexual boasting but also a tenderness towards women. Many others, in the true spirit of the blues, were about deceit, abandonment and mistreatment such as "Got the Blues", "Black Snake Moan" and "Broke and Hungry". Jefferson also had an affinity for prisoners, perhaps because his visual disability also imprisoned him at times, and he often sang about courtroom scenes. His success allowed him to live to a reasonable standard but he remained a wanderer at heart and failed to settle down. He moved around the Delta, to Chicago, Texas and the coal camps of West Virginia, and was in great demand. Although Jefferson's recording career was short, at only four years, he recorded close to a hundred songs. In 1929, on the way back from a gig in Chicago, he is said to have frozen to death alone in the snow while waiting for a lift back to Texas.

Jefferson had a great influence on many other musicians; his songs have been covered by Bob Dylan and the band Jefferson Airplane took their name from him.

One of the bluesmen he inspired in his lifetime was Lightnin' Hopkins.

BIOGRAPHY:

Lightnin' Hopkins

Sam Hopkins was born in March 1912 in Centreville, Texas. He first learned to play a homemade cigar-box "guitar" and then his brother taught him to play a real one. He left home early and went travelling, inspired by his mentor Blind Lemon Jefferson, whom he would meet up with on the road. His formative years were spent playing his acoustic guitar in the juke joints and barn dances around his home state. Hopkins' first recording experiences were on Texas Alexander's records for the Okeh label; Alexander was his cousin. Hopkins also spent a short time working on a chain gang in the late 1930s (an experience he would recapture later in a number of his songs such as "Penitentiary Blues"). He had a very astute way of looking at life, which was reflected in his lyrics. He earned the title "Lightnin'" after working as a duet alongside the barrelhouse pianist "Thunder" Smith. The duo recorded in the late 1940s, having impressed a record label executive who worked out of Los Angeles. However, it was Lightnin's relationship with his guitar and his sparse and quirky style that impressed the most and the duo only made two sessions together for the Aladdin label before it was decided that Hopkins was better as a solo artist. Lightnin' made a number of other records on his own for the same label, as well as for the Imperial and Gold Star labels. In the early 1950s, the audience for Hopkins' country blues was mainly black American.

It was not until 1959 that he was rediscovered by a mainstream audience with his recording *The Roots of Lightnin' Hopkins* and his career took off across the whole of America. Hundreds of recording sessions followed throughout the 1960s, and he was very much in demand for his folksy live performances as well. Although he mainly played acoustic guitar he ventured into the realms of electric guitar as well, maintaining the dialogue between guitar and voice.

From 1964 until 1977 he went on world tours which covered Britain and Europe. Sadly, his declining health meant that he could not maintain the pace and he was forced to retire. He died in January 1982.

"When I play a guitar I play it from my heart and soul"

(LIGHTNIN' HOPKINS)

The blues always attracted unusual characters and perhaps one of the most unusual and most mysterious of these was Leadbelly. His violent flares of temper often put him in prison. Fortunately, his song-writing talent, along with his baritone voice and 12-string guitar playing, was able to win through and his influence can still be heard in music from the country blues to rock bands today.

Above: Lightnin' Hopkins – the President of Country Blues.

BIOGRAPHY:

Leadbelly

Huddie William Ledbetter was born in January in the mid-1880s in Louisiana. His exact date of birth is unknown because he often gave conflicting information which made it difficult to be certain of much of what he said. His family moved to Texas in his early years. The first instrument he learned to play was the accordion but by the time he was in his early teens he had taught himself the guitar. He left home in 1901 to earn his living at various odd jobs whilst supplementing his income as a wandering minstrel, playing in and around Dallas and Fort Worth, Texas. It was in Dallas that he teamed up with Blind Lemon Jefferson and learned to play the 12-string guitar, the instrument for which he became renowned.

In 1905 he had the first of two children with Margaret Coleman. In 1916 he married Eletha Henderson although this was shortlived because in 1917 he was convicted of murder under the name of William Boyd, a name he had assumed because he had already escaped prison once before for another assault charge. It was during his time in prison that he earned the nickname of Leadbelly. Various theories abound as to how this arose, including that he took a shot to the stomach and lived to tell the tale. He served seven years of his 33-year hard labour sentence before he was pardoned by the governor, having written a song in honour of him. He spent five years on the "outside", again playing

music to supplement his income gained from odd jobs. However, in 1930 he once again went to prison on a charge of assault with intent to murder. Justice for black Americans at the time was somewhat limited and a fair trial, especially if the other party was white, as in this case, was unlikely. Fortunately, he gained the interest of John Lomax, a folklorist, who was collecting spirituals, ballads and work songs from the southern prisons. Lomax made numerous recordings with Leadbelly at the prison and was so enamoured with his find that he was able to get Leadbelly an early pardon in 1934, by again using the tactic of flattering the prison governor with a petition song written for him. This was to be the B-side of "Goodnight Irene", a song Leadbelly first sang for Lomax in 1933 in Angola Prison camp but was commercially recorded in 1935. It was to become one of the folk anthems of the 1960s and has been recorded by Jimi Hendrix, Brian Ferry, Little Richard and Van Morrison amongst others.

In 1935 Leadbelly was taken to New York by Lomax to perform and he gained a national audience. Indeed Leadbelly, ever the performer, played on his southern black background, especially for the northern white audiences who were intrigued by his quaint "negro" ways as he passed his hat around after performances. However, he was also involved in the political rights movement and won a great deal of respect from a

number of folk musicians including Woody Guthrie over the next decade, and many artists sought to accompany him on recordings and on stage.

He died in 1949 from the fatal neuromuscular disease of lateral sclerosis and was buried in his native Louisiana.

Above: Leadbelly – prison bluesman.

BIOGRAPHY:

Ray Charles

Ray Charles Robinson was born into extreme poverty on 23 September 1930 in Albany, Georgia. By the age of seven the disease glaucoma had taken his sight away completely. He learned to read and write music in Braille and by the time he left school he was proficient in several musical instruments. His mother died when he was only 15 and Charles was forced to make his own way. He soon began drifting around the Florida music scene, picking up work whenever he could until he moved to Seattle.

In Seattle he began to make a name for himself in several nightclubs. In 1949 he began recording. In 1952 he was signed up by Atlantic Records and recorded amongst others "Mess Around", "Losing Hand" and "It Should Have Been Me". This was his early R&B era.

He next began working with Guitar Slim who combined blues guitar with a gospel style. Charles arranged Slim's million-selling single "Things That I Used To Do" and in 1954 released "I Got A Woman", which became one of the great blues classics. The record achieved both artistic and commercial success and inspired other recordings such as "This Little Girl of Mine", "Talkin' 'Bout You" and "Don't Let the Sun Catch You Crying". In 1959 Charles recorded what was to become one of the all-time great encore numbers called "What'd I Say", a song that has been performed by countless bands and singers in venues around the world. Charles was equally adept at slow ballads, shown to great effect in "Drown In My Own Tears" and "I Believe to My Soul", both recorded that same year. In 1959 he left Atlantic and joined ABC Records which allowed him both financial and artistic freedom.

In 1960 Charles recorded "Georgia On My Mind" and "Hit the Road Jack" which established him as an international artist. In 1962 he released the massive selling album *Modern Sounds in Country and Western Music*, from which came the million-selling single "I Can't Stop Loving You". As the 60s progressed Ray Charles began to move away from his blues and Jazz roots into more middle-of-the-road pop music. He covered Beatles' songs and worked with Stevie Wonder and Randy Newman. During the 1980s his music became more country flavoured. In 1980 he appeared in the movie *The Blues Brothers*. He also appeared on the charity single "We Are the World" in 1985 by the US equivalent of Band Aid.

Charles has been widely imitated, particularly by many of the white blues artists such as Eric Burdon, Van Morrison and Joe Cocker. He has received numerous awards and accolades throughout his career and in 1987 received a Grammy Lifetime Achievement award.

In 2000 Charles made a return to jazz. As a singer, composer, arranger and pianist he is no less than a genius. His ability to cross over into a variety of musical territories is the envy of many musicians and he has performed jazz, blues, country and rock with ease. Ray Charles is considered by many to be one of the great talents of the last century.

Above: Ray Charles.

EAST COAST BLUES

East Coast blues, also known as Piedmont blues, has its own easily recognised style and evolved differently from Delta and Texas blues. It has a more "white" country influence and a definite songster quality about it as there was an important vaudeville circuit in the area. It also has a definite flavour of ragtime but, whereas ragtime is piano-based, the guitar is the dominant instrument in East Coast blues. It is characterised by a finger-picking technique which is thought to stem from the black American banjo-playing style where the thumb plays rhythm on the bass strings and two, three or even four fingers pick the others. This requires a huge amount of dexterity and many of the proponents were multi-instrumentalists. Unfortunately, this style does not lend itself readily to amplification but it was to enormously influence the folk music scene of the 1950s and 1960s.

One of the many things that blues has done is change the political climate. When the blues first started to be recorded, it was released as "race music" and only black Americans listened to it. Fortunately the spread of blues music encouraged people to stop fearing each other because of skin colour and helped break down cultural and political barriers across the world. The repressed were given a voice and one of the main protagonists of folk blues was Brownie McGhee.

BIOGRAPHY:

Brownie McGhee

Walter Brown McGhee was born in November 1915 in Knoxville, Tennessee. He and his family lived and worked on a farm and it was through his father, who played at local parties and dances, that he first learned to appreciate music. His fiddle-playing uncle and mother were also interested in music. At the age of four McGhee contracted polio which left him with a slight limp. This affected his ability to assist on the farm for a time and so he was able to dedicate himself to learning musical instruments. He was playing both the banjo and guitar by the age of eight and also added the piano and organ. In his mid-teens he left school and went on the road as a wandering minstrel, playing carnivals and camps.

In the Depression years he returned to his family's farm to assist them but by the end of the 1930s he was back travelling around the tobacco industry towns of North Carolina, playing and hustling for a living. It was whilst he was in North Carolina that he met up with Blind Boy Fuller, the steel guitarist. Fuller had a manager, J B Long, who also worked for Okeh Records, and together Fuller and McGhee made such an impression on him that they were sent to Chicago to record. They released a single featuring Fuller on the A-side and McGhee's "Me and My Dog" on the B-side. In 1940 the Fuller/McGhee pairing was set to work together again but Fuller died under mysterious circumstances in 1941. This left McGhee to work on his own and he recorded a song "The Death of Blind Boy Fuller" which he dedicated to his partner, even playing Fuller's steel guitar on the track and recording it under the name of Fuller. That guitar was to remain with him for some time, having been given to him by Long after Fuller's death. McGhee for a time made recordings under a variety of pseudonyms. In 1941, eager to work under his own name again, McGhee paired up with Sonny Terry and the duo made a number of recordings. This brought them success and in the early 1940s they moved to Harlem, New York, even staying with Leadbelly for a time. McGhee met Bill Broonzy through Leadbelly at this time. Alan Lomax, the folklorist also met up with McGhee and interviewed him as well as recorded him for his archives. McGhee was always happy to oblige with requests to ensure that his folk songs and tales were available for future generations.

McGhee set up a blues school in New York and played in the politically groundbreaking Greenwich Village coffee houses. The Terry/McGhee partnership worked for the next three decades, playing on the folk festival circuit with the aforementioned Leadbelly, Woody Guthrie, Burl Ives and the Weavers, and brought folk blues to a predominantly white audience. In 1960 he and Terry worked with Lightnin' Hopkins on an album. He also made a number of solo recordings and worked on Broadway in productions such as *Cat on a Hot Tin Roof*.

He died in February 1996 from stomach cancer, ten years after his partner Sonny Terry.

Above: Brownie McGhee — the Travellin' Folk Bluesman and his partner Sonny Terry.

BIOGRAPHY:

Sonny Terry

Sanford Terrell was born in October 1911 in Greensboro, North Carolina. He had two accidents, each of which caused damage to his eyes so that by the age of 16 he was blind. Fortunately he was able to turn this to his advantage. He began to concentrate on his musical aspirations and was soon performing at carnivals and medicine shows. In 1937 he joined up with Blind Boy Fuller and the pair played and recorded on the Durham East Coast blues scene. After Fuller's death he paired up with Brownie McGhee and the two hit the big time on New York folk blues scene. Terry also worked as a solo artist and appeared in Broadway productions such as *Finian's Rainbow*.

Strangely Terry and McGhee, although they performed well together in their professional lives, had problems with their relationship on a personal basis and would even argue mid-performance. By the early 1970s they had completely stopped speaking to each other and relied on other musicians that they worked with to act as intermediaries instead. Eventually they parted company although both continued to work as solo artists. In 1984 Terry made an album *Whoopin'* with Johnny Winter. In 1986 he died whilst in New York.

One of the major exponents of the Piedmont blues sound was Blind Blake. He is often considered the mystery man of the blues because so little is known about his life.

Above: Terry and McGhee performing together.

Biography:

Blind Blake

Arthur Blake was born in the 1890s in Jacksonville, Florida. Little is known of his early life except that he was blind and earned his living as a wandering musician on the East Coast of the USA, at various times known as Arthur Phelps, Arthur Blake and Blind Blake. In 1926 he made his first recording "West Coast Blues" for the Paramount label in Chicago. This established his career alongside the likes of Blind Lemon Jefferson. He made over 80 recordings for Paramount including some on which he worked with Ma Rainey and Papa Charlie Jackson, with whom he made the album *Blind Blake and Papa Charlie Talk*. Although he was a master of Piedmont blues he also blended ragtime and jazz into his repertoire.

In the early 1930s Blake worked in the vaudeville show *Happy Go Lucky*. In 1932 when Paramount closed its doors, Blake disappeared into obscurity. A year later he died, although to this day his exact cause of death is unknown.

Above: Blind Blake – the Mysterious Bluesman.

BIOGRAPHY:

Blind Willie McTell

William Samuel McTell was born in 1901 in Thomson, Georgia. He lost his sight in childhood, but his mother taught him to play the guitar and fortunately he became adept at reading and writing in Braille which allowed him to be an accomplished music theorist.

In 1927 he made his first record for the Atlantic label as Blind Willie McTell. It featured his sweet 12-string playing and his clean, crisp voice. However, he was notorious for working under a variety of names and signed himself to a number of labels. His name McTell is believed to have come from a mispronunciation but he also worked as Barrel House Sammy, Blind Sammie and many others. In 1934 he married his wife Kate, a nurse who spent her time waiting for him to return from his travels.

In all McTell did 14 recording sessions resulting in over 120 songs. Strangely he never achieved a hit record and from 1937 to 1948 he spent his time "rambling" up and down the East Coast of the USA playing live gigs rather than in the studio. The recording partner that he worked with the most during his career was Curley Weaver but in 1950 he played his last session with him. Over the next few years McTell reluctantly recorded; sadly most of these tapes were never to be heard by the public because they were placed in storage where they were damaged. In 1957 McTell gave up his musical career altogether and turned to the church and became a preacher. In August 1959 he died from a brain haemorrhage. Since his death many musicians from Bob Dylan to Taj Mahal have paid homage to him and his music.

The Lomax family folklorists and ethnomusicologists are essential to blues history. Without them much of what we know about blues music would have been lost forever. Thankfully they had the vision and foresight to meet with and record early blues artists as well as transcribe folk and blues songs.

BIOGRAPHY:

The Lomax Family

John Avery Lomax was born in Goodman, Mississippi in September 1867. He was raised at the family farm on the Texas frontier. He began his career by teaching in rural schools and then entered the University of Texas in 1895 to study English Literature. He arrived at the university with a book of cowboy songs that he had written down in his childhood but unfortunately, this early interest in folk songs was not considered academic enough for the professors. After graduation he worked at the university as registrar and personal secretary to the president.

In 1903 Lomax began teaching at Texas A and M University and settled down with his new wife Bess Brown Lomax. However, quiet country living did not suit John Avery for long and in 1907 he went to Harvard as a graduate, where he was encouraged to revive his interest in cowboy songs. He obtained his MA and then resumed his teaching position back in Texas. He was awarded a grant to research and collect further cowboy songs which he published as an anthology called *Cowboy Songs and Other Frontier Ballads* in 1910. That same year he established the Texan branch of the American Folklore Society. He was also offered an administrative position at the University of Texas and over the next seven years

continued his research into American folk songs as well as undertaking lecture tours, ably assisted by his wife and children. Unfortunately, in 1917, along with six other faculty members, he was fired as a result of an internal political battle and so he moved to Chicago and began working as a banker. Shortly afterwards his dismissal was rescinded but he was not prepared to return to his former role. During the next 15 years Lomax divided his time between banking and researching folk music.

In 1931 tragedy struck the family when Bess died suddenly leaving her four children in the care of John. The following year John Lomax Jr encouraged his father to start a new series of lecture tours and the whole family went back out on the road again. In June 1932 they arrived in Washington to work on an all-inclusive anthology of American ballads and folk songs. The following year, assisted by his son Alan, he made his first recording field trip for the American Library of Congress. The Archive of American Folk Song in the Library of Congress already contained a collection of commercial phonograph and wax cylinder field recordings of folk songs. For the next ten years, John Avery, assisted by all his children and his second wife Ruby Terrell Lomax, travelled the length and breadth of

Left: Blind Willie McTell – the Statesman of the Blues.

the USA recording artists such as Leadbelly, Woody Guthrie, Muddy Waters, Molly Jackson and Brownie McGhee as well as touring prison farms. They collected reels, work songs and blues songs from prisoners. The prisons were excellent locations for field work because many of the long-term inmates were untouched by the culture of the modern world. Here the Lomax family could find authentic blues.

In 1934 Lomax was named Honorary Consultant and Curator of the Archive of American Folk Song. In 1936 he served as an advisor on folklore, collecting for both the Historical Records Survey and the Federal Writers' Project. He gathered the narratives of ex-slaves who reminisced on their early years as well as describing the field hollers, shouts and arhoolies that had evolved into the blues.

After his death in 1948 his son Alan took over his life's work. Alan Lomax was born in 1915. In 1933 he first began to accompany his father and in 1939 he wrote and directed an American radio series called *American Folk Songs* which was to air over a 26-week period. During World War II he continued to do specialist music broadcasts.

In 1946 Alan Lomax recorded Memphis Slim, Sonny Boy Williamson and Big Bill Broonzy. This recording was actually released as an album called *Blues in the Mississippi Night*. In 1949 he moved to England and began recording extensively the traditional music of England, Ireland and

Scotland and made numerous television and radio broadcasts on the BBC. These recordings became the basis of *Folk Songs of Great Britain* which was a ten-record series released in 1961. After travelling around Europe and recording the folk music of Italy and Spain he returned to the USA in 1959 where he embarked on a major field trip recording the living traditions in Virginia, Kentucky, Alabama, Mississippi, Tennessee, Arkansas and the Georgia Sea Islands. In 1962 he toured the West Indies and gathered traditional Caribbean music as well as recording the songs of the Hindu community in Trinidad. In 1989 Lomax developed the Global Jukebox which is an interactive multimedia museum of music and dance of the world. He also set about creating a statistical system to categorise various forms of song and dance from around the world. In 1993 he was to receive awards for his book *The Land Where the Blues Began*. He continued to study folk music until his retirement in 1996.

Sadly, the world lost Alan Lomax in July 2002.

Left: Alan Lomax.

URBAN BLUES

"The blues? It's the mother of American music. That's what it is, the source."

(B B KING)

THE GREAT MIGRATION

In the 1920s many of the black musicians from the Mississippi Delta area migrated northwards, utilising the railroads, in search of employment, higher pay and a better way of life. Even though the Civil War had been fought some 60 years or so earlier, racism still ran rife in the southern areas of the United States. Many families relied on sharecropping for their income and the musicians relied on the audiences in the juke joints and roadhouses in which they played. When these audiences began to head north in search of opportunity, the musicians followed them. The main employment in the south was agricultural, whereas in the north it was generally industrial. Many urban areas were settled by migratory southerners. While Harlem became the Mecca for jazz, it was the Windy City of Chicago in Michigan that became the new home of the blues, although many other cities, such as Detroit, also played a large role in its development. The sound of the country blues changed to match its new city surroundings and thus the urban blues was born.

During his long career Tampa Red was to write many blues standards including "It Hurts Me Too", "Love Her with a Feeling", "Sweet Black Angel" and "Don't You Lie to Me" which are still covered to this day. He helped the blues make the transition from country style to urban Chicago blues.

Above: In the 1920s many of the black musicians from the Mississippi Delta area migrated northwards, utilising the railroads, in search of employment,

BIOGRAPHY:

Tampa Red

Hudson Woodbridge was born in January 1904 in Smithville, Georgia but was raised in Tampa, Florida and it was there he earned his nickname. He was known as the Guitar Wizard because of his precise bottleneck blues style. In 1925 he began playing with Georgia Tom Dorsey in Chicago, touring the black theatre circuit. The pair made their first record "It's Tight Like That" which was recorded on Vocalion Records in late 1928 and it became a hit. He and Dorsey recorded together extensively until 1932 when Dorsey moved over onto the gospel circuit. Red also recorded with his own Hokum Jug Band. In 1934 he signed with Victor Records and ceased touring outside Chicago. During this time many of his songs became popular hits, performed by his Chicago Five. He was also an accomplished pianist.

In the late 1940s Red led a band whose rhythms were the precursor of the post-war Chicago sound. His wife Frances was also his business manager and ran their home as both a lodging house and rehearsal centre for other blues singers on tour such as Big Bill Broonzy. When Frances died in the mid-1950s, Red took to excessive drinking in order to cope with his grief. In 1960 he made a small comeback and recorded two solo albums for Bluesville. However, he retired in the 1970s and in 1974 moved to a nursing home where he died in 1981.

Another of the blues' most influential female artists was Memphis Minnie, whose roots were in country blues but who made a successful transition onto the Chicago and Memphis blues scenes at a time when women blues singers had fallen out of favour with the public.

Above: Tampa Red — the Guitar Wizard.

BIOGRAPHY:
Memphis Minnie

Lizzie Douglas was born in Algiers, Louisiana in June 1897. At the age of nine she and her family moved to the town of Walls near Memphis. In her early teens, having learned to play guitar and banjo she began busking on Memphis street corners and then joined the Ringling Brothers Circus, where she was called Kid Douglas.

In the 1920s she moved onto the Memphis blues scene and in 1929 was discovered by a talent scout for Columbia Records. She recorded her first song that year called "Bumblebee" under the name of Memphis Minnie. She also wrote songs – Led Zeppelin immortalised an adaptation of her 1929 song "When the Levee Breaks" which was written about the dangers that plantation workers faced during floods that could sweep away their homes and their lives. In 1930, she and her husband Kansas Joe McCoy moved to Chicago and, along with Bill Broonzy and Tampa Red, helped the country blues style move to an urban setting. Whilst in Chicago, she recorded over a hundred sides for a number of labels including Vocalion, Decca and Bluebird. She was also known for her guitar duels against Broonzy, Tampa Red and Muddy Waters. In the mid-1950s her health began to fail and she retired to Memphis. She died of a stroke in August 1973 whilst staying in a nursing home.

"If it keeps on raining, the levee's going to break,

If it keeps on raining, the levee's going to break,

When the levee breaks I'll have no place to stay."

MEMPHIS MINNIE – "WHEN THE LEVEE BREAKS"

When the Great Depression hit during the mid-1920s and 1930s, record sales plummeted considerably. This slowed the level of migration but many innovative and ground-breaking recordings were still made at this time, particularly on the Paramount label run by Ink Williams, such as those of Big Bill Broonzy.

Above: Memphis Minnie – the Hoodoo Lady.

Big Bill Broonzy

William Lee Conley Broonzy was born in Scott County, Mississippi in June 1883. As a child he helped his family who were sharecroppers and learned to play the fiddle from his uncle. When he was 14 he began busking at local dances and picnics.

During the years 1912 to 1917 he worked both as a preacher and as a violinist, as well as serving in the US Army during World War I. After the war, he decided to make his living as a professional musician and in 1924 he moved to Chicago. His guitar teacher was Papa Charlie Jackson and by the 1930s he had become one of the major artists on the Chicago blues scene, performing with many top blues artists such as Tampa Red, Sonny Boy Williamson and Memphis Minnie.

In 1938, Broonzy performed at John Hammond's famous *From Spirituals to Swing* concert in Carnegie Hall, New York City. For him this was his first performance in front of a white audience and the newspapers began to refer to him as "Big Bill" Broonzy. He recorded over 260 blues songs over the next five decades and travelled throughout the States and Europe, where he became highly respected. With the arrival of electric blues through artists like Muddy Waters, Big Bill's brand of blues declined in popularity but rather than retire he changed his style. In 1951 he toured Europe where he performed standard blues as well as traditional folk tunes and spirituals. The following year he also toured Europe with the pianist Blind John Davis. In 1955 Broonzy published his autobiography which was one of the first about a bluesman. In 1957 he was diagnosed with throat cancer. However, he continued to perform until his death in August 1958.

"I'm just like an old rooster, out way out here on a hill

I'm just like an old rooster, out way out here on a hill

People I'm done scratchin', ooh Lord, Big Bill is just tryin' to live"

(BIG BILL BROONZY)

Above: Big Bill Broonzy.

STOMPIN' BLUES

New Orleans is considered to be the heartland of the birth of the phenomenon called jazz music. Jazz grew up at the same time as the blues and arose from the same people and from the same African traditions. However, whereas pure blues featured a solo artist with a guitar, jazz took the form and rearranged it into orchestral music with the guitar right in the background and the horns up front. Jazz, like the blues, moved up the Mississippi to the urban areas. Many black American musicians who had cut their teeth in the juke joints and levee parties on the banks of the Mississippi moved to these urban areas and added their musical talents to the melting pot. The blues evolved into jazz. Many jazz songs such as "Beale Street Blues" and "St Louis Blues" are in fact foxtrots and Dixieland dance music. Many of the great jazz men of the time were also known as bluesmen. The genre reached its peak with the internationally famous *Rhapsody in Blue* by George Gershwin which mixed the blue notes of the blues with the orchestral arrangements of jazz and classical music and took it into the concert halls of the world.

During the 1920s and 1930s this orchestral style of blues music filled the dance halls and juke joints of the urban sprawl on a Saturday night with jivers, jumpers, hoppers and stompers out on the town to celebrate.

POST-WAR BLUES

The economic climate after World War II caused further demographic changes in the United States and even more people, particularly black Americans, moved from the country to the city. Whereas the pre-war sound tended to be acoustic with either soloists, duets or simple orchestrations featuring acoustic guitar, acoustic

bass, harmonica and simple percussion instruments, such as the washboard, the post-war sound moved into electric territory. Electric guitars, drum kits and saxophones featured heavily in the new, brasher, urban sound. Most instruments were amplified using the newly available technology that was being developed in the music and recording industry. Even the humble harmonica was hooked up to microphones as the blues gained mainstream popularity.

One of the musicians who played timeless yet technically innovative music which crossed the boundaries between jazz and blues was T-Bone Walker. He is also considered the first bluesman to plug his guitar into an amplifier, thus paving the way for electric blues.

Above: Beale Street in Memphis gave its name to "Beale Street Blues".

BIOGRAPHY:

T-Bone Walker

Aaron Thibeaux Walker was born in May 1910 in Linden, Texas. He was of Cherokee Indian descent and his stepfather played in many local bands. Although he first learned to play banjo it was not long before he switched to guitar and among his teachers were Chuck Richardson and the jazz guitarist Charlie Christian. He was also heavily influenced by Ma Rainey. In the 1930s, Walker began to develop his own musical style by leaving behind the rural blues of his early years and moving toward the sophistication of big band jazz.

In 1942, he recorded his first standards "I've Got a Break Baby" and "Mean Old World" with Capitol Records. During the 1940s he returned to the West Coast and recorded for Black & White Records. Some of the top jazz musicians of the day supported him on these sessions, playing for the first time in a blues setting. These sessions showed his ability to play anything from the straight blues of "Stormy Monday" to jives such as "Hypin Woman".

During the early 1950s he recorded sessions for Imperial Records incorporating a harder sound. In 1955 he moved to Atlantic Records where he teamed up with jazz guitarist Barney Kessel amongst others. In 1960s America the blues audiences were beginning to take less interest in his style of music. Fortunately Walker was booked into a European tour and gained a new following. In the early 1970s he recorded a Grammy award-winning album for Polydor Records. Sadly he was involved in a car accident and life on the road began to take its toll upon his health. In 1974 he suffered a stroke and he died in 1975.

Chicago was the main city for blues musicians to work in and perhaps the most famous location in Chicago blues history at that period was 2120 South Michigan Avenue, the offices of Chess Records. Throughout the 1950s it was Chess that dominated the market in blues music.

Above: T-Bone Walker – the first electric blues guitarist.

CHESS RECORDS

Chess Records epitomised the sound of Chicago blues and was formed by two Polish-American brothers, Leonard and Philip Chess. They originally bought into Aristocrat Records, a label that had been formed a short time before by Evelyn Aaron and her husband. Leonard Chess owned a nightclub called the Macomba which headlined stars such as Ella Fitzgerald and Billy Eckstine and the Aristocrat label reflected this sophisticated club style jazz. Aristocrat soon became the lynchpin of a new style of blues, taking its roots from the Mississippi Delta and adding a modern urban brashness. The two brothers were extremely well-connected in terms of clubs and radio presence. Phil ran the clubs and offices whereas Leonard ran the recording studios and radio stations as well as being their talent scout. The Chess label, which was Aristocrat's successor, soon became the primary recording focus for the entire post-war Chicago blues movement.

The Chess label itself achieved its individuality and therefore its prominence through the work of Muddy Waters. In April 1948 Waters cut his first record for Aristocrat: "I Can't Be Satisfied" and "I Feel Like Going Home" which was pure Mississippi Delta country blues. In 1949 the Chess brothers bought out the Aarons and in 1950 changed the name of the company to Chess. Waters' definitive growl became the hallmark of Chess's style. The label soon became stocked with new stars drawn to Chicago and whose first taste of musical success was often in Muddy Waters' houseband. These included Jimmy Rogers, Willie Dixon, Rosco Gordon, Rufus Thomas and Little Walter Jacobs, the harmonica wizard who revolutionised the role of the harmonica in Chicago blues. Other essential Chess artists were Ike Turner, Big Bill Broonzy, Washboard Sam, Memphis Minnie, Sonny Boy Williamson, Bo Diddley and Chuck Berry.

Above: Phil Chess (left) and Marshall Chess with Willie Dixon (seated).

In 1963, Chess had its own radio station dedicated to the blues – WVON, which is still running and servicing its community in Chicago. Sadly, in 1969 Leonard Chess died. Earlier that year he and his brother had sold the company to GRT and there was a noticeable drop in the quality of the label's output. In 1975 Chess closed its doors forever but left behind a back catalogue of blues songs that are still loved to this day.

One of the most prolific writers of blues songs was Willie Dixon who worked through the Chess label. He penned over 500 songs which were recorded by not only blues artists but others like Elvis Presley. Dixon used to say of himself that "I am the blues" and certainly without him it is likely that the blues as we know it today would not exist.

Above: Leonard Chess.

BIOGRAPHY:

Willie Dixon

Dixon was born in Mississippi in July 1915 and it was through the influence of his mother Daisy that his songwriting skills developed. She would speak by rhyming and her son soon followed suit, making lyrics up on the spot. During his school years he learned to play piano with a local musician Little Brother Montgomery. He also sang bass in local gospel choirs.

He moved to Chicago and had a stint as a boxer. It was not until he met with Leonard "Baby Doo" Caston that he turned his attention to music on a professional basis. Their vocal harmony/blues/jazz band the Five Breezes, later cut down to a trio as the Big Three Trio, made a number of recordings throughout the 1940s, interrupted only by Dixon going to prison for ten months when he dodged the wartime draft, and a stint with Dixon's own band the upbeat Four Jumps of Jive. By the late 1940s Dixon had involved himself with Chess Records so much so that he barely performed with Caston anymore and in 1951 Dixon was working full-time for Chess.

At Chess he acted as a producer, A&R man, session musician (playing bass on many recordings), songwriter, and even, on occasion, recorded under his own name. He was responsible for the Chicago sound as exemplified by Chess and Cobra records. The skills of Bo Diddley, Muddy Waters and Chuck Berry were all honed by Dixon in the studio on Dixon-penned tracks such as "Hoochie Coochie Man" and "You Can't Judge a Book by Its Cover". In the 1960s Dixon put together many of the American Folk Blues Festival tours of Europe that American bluesmen undertook, and so brought the blues to a new audience.

In 1971 Dixon left Chess and was forced into taking complex legal action in order to regain copyright control over many of the songs he had written in their long relationship. He put together his own record labels of Spoonful and Yambo and also formed the Blues Heaven Foundation to promote awareness of the blues and ensure that black artists were remunerated properly.

He died at the beginning of 1992.

Howlin' Wolf was a seminal figure in the development of the Chicago blues style. His fierce growling voice combined with his trademark howl epitomised the primitive energy of the country blues of the Delta. He was one of the first to make the transition from country to urban-style blues. Literally hundreds of artists have claimed him as a major influence and hundreds have recorded his songs.

Above: Willie Dixon – the Wang Dang Doodle Man.

BIOGRAPHY:

Howlin' Wolf

Chester Arthur Burnett, known as Howlin' Wolf, was born in June 1910 in the area around West Point and Aberdeen, Mississippi. When he was 13 his family moved to Ruleville. For his 18th birthday his father gave him a guitar and subsequently he met Charley Patton. Patton took Burnett under his wing as his protégé and taught him the Delta blues style. Wolf's performance was very influenced by Patton's wildly dramatic method of performing.

In 1933, the Burnett family moved to Parkin, Arkansas where Burnett learned to play the harmonica from Sonny Boy Williamson who was by then his brother-in-law. The pair began to play the bars as a team. In 1941 Burnett was drafted for World War II and, following his discharge in 1945, he returned to Parkin as a farmer for a couple of years. He also met his wife Lillie in the mid-1940s.

In 1948 he moved to West Memphis, Tennessee and formed a band of his own, beginning a serious career as a professional musician. His big break came through a West Memphis radio station called KWEM on which he performed a weekly show and he began using the name Howlin' Wolf which suited his howling singing style. His radio success led him to record in 1950. His Chess 78rpm record "How Many More Years/Moanin' at Midnight" sold 60,000 copies which ensured it was

a hit. In 1952 Wolf signed a contract with Chess and recorded exclusively with the label for the remainder of his career. During the 1950s he performed both in the studio and in clubs around Chicago. During the mid-1960s he toured Europe extensively as part of a Chess blues Revival show, although by then he had adapted his sound to that of rock 'n' roll. Many British bands began recording his songs and asked him to be the warm-up act on their tours, particularly the Rolling Stones. At 6'6" and weighing close to 300lbs, Howlin' Wolf had a commanding and intense stage presence, capable of bringing the house down. He often dropped to the floor of the stage as if possessed by spirits, all the while howling and hollering.

In 1971 he worked with an all-star line-up of British bluesmen such as Eric Clapton, Stevie Winwood and Charlie Watts on his *London Sessions*. Sadly, towards the end of his career he was plagued with heart problems and was also involved in a car crash in which his kidneys were damaged. He died from renal failure on 10 January 1976 in a Chicago hospital.

The blues song "Mr James" by John Mayall was a tribute to Elmore James. His influence was enormous and his style was legendary. Many artists sought to copy it, particularly Jeremy Spencer of Fleetwood Mac. His other devotees included Jimi Hendrix, Brian Jones of the Rolling Stones and more recent bands such as the Black Crowes.

Above: Howlin' Wolf – the Big Man of the Blues.

BIOGRAPHY:

Elmore James

Elmore James was born in January 1918, in Richmond, Mississippi. His first guitar was a National. His early years were spent playing in the Mississippi juke joints with his cousin, but for the most part he performed on his own.

In 1937 James moved to Greenville, Mississippi and became a close friend of Sonny Boy Williamson. He learned to play "Dust My Broom" and knew Robert Johnson, although when Johnson was murdered James decided to leave the area as he feared the same fate. Between 1943 and 1945 James served with the US Army in the Pacific. On his return he became a regular performer on KFFA's *King Biscuit Time* radio show. Owing to his association with Williamson, he secured a recording contract in 1951 and moved to Chicago where he recorded "Dust My Broom" as his debut single. Although it met with great success, James had not agreed to its release as he had believed his recording session to be a rehearsal.

In 1952 he signed to another record label. He fronted several groups all bearing the name the Broomdusters. James's slide guitar and passionate vocals were to become his trademark. Other famous recordings followed, such as "Bleeding Heart" and "Shake Your Moneymaker". However, his shyness and a lack of credible sales for his records meant he moved back and forth between the Delta and Chicago for the rest of the 1950s seeking employment and by the late 1950s was working as a DJ. In 1957 he was diagnosed with a heart problem which also affected his ability to work. In the early 1960s he was signed to a new label but it took over a year before he was given the opportunity to record due to problems with the musicians' union. Unfortunately James never made it into the studio as he died on 23 May 1963 having suffered a heart attack. He was never to know the impact his brief recording career and slide guitar style had on musicians such as Jeremy Spencer or John Mayall.

Muddy Waters came to exemplify the sound of the blues and, through his use of amplification, came to influence a whole generation of guitarists such as Keith Richards from the Rolling Stones. Long John Baldry, the Graham Bond Organisation, Alexis Korner, Blues Incorporated and The Rolling Stones all pay tribute to his influence.

Above: Elmore James.

Muddy Waters

McKinley Morganfield, known as Muddy Waters, was born in April 1915 at Rolling Fork, Mississippi, and raised in Clarksdale. In his early teens he learned the harmonica but at the age of 17 he was to pick up the guitar. He was taught by the legendary Son House and through him mastered the country blues guitar and the bottleneck slide technique.

In 1943 Waters moved to Chicago and was befriended by Big Bill Broonzy who helped him into the parties and clubs there. Although Waters had made recordings for Columbia they were not released and he was having to work part-time at odd jobs. However, by 1948 Waters was using amplified electric guitar and signed a successful recording contract with Chess Records. His early recordings were in the Mississippi Delta style but he soon evolved this further. By 1951 he was utilising a full backing band and some of the musicians who passed through its ranks were Otis Spann, Jimmy Rogers, Little Walter, Shaky Horton and James Cotton. These talented musicians ensured that the Muddy Waters Blues Band was one of Chicago's most influential. Their recordings of "Hoochie Coochie Man", "Got My Mojo Working" and "You Need Love" (infamously reworked by Led Zeppelin as "Whole Lotta Love") amongst others are seminal.

Throughout the 1950s the Waters sound became more urbanised and this was also reflected in the lyrics. He gained an international following in 1958 when he toured Britain and although, he received criticism for his use of amplification which went against his earliest country roots, his effect on a new generation of guitarists was enormous. His rich and deep singing voice also made an impact.

In the 1960s he was joined by Paul Butterfield and Mike Bloomfield and appeared at the Band's *Last Waltz* concert. Waters made a number of recordings in the 1970s. His most inspired series of collaborations was with the guitarist Johnny Winter who arranged four superb albums on the Blue Sky label, which faithfully recaptured the excitement of Waters' early releases.

Although the 1980s saw Waters adopt a slower pace he still made live guest appearances with other artists, mainly from the British blues scene. Indeed his last live performance was with Eric Clapton in 1982. Muddy Waters died peacefully at his home in April 1983.

Above: Muddy Waters.

BIOGRAPHY:

Sonny Boy Williamson

Rice Ford was the second bluesman to use the name Sonny Boy Williamson. He was born illegitimately to Millie Ford on 4 December 1899 in Helena, Arkansas. Later he changed his name to that of his stepfather and became Rice Miller. His early youth found him wandering throughout the south, playing with the top blues artists of the time such as Elmore James, Howlin' Wolf and Robert Johnson. He married Howlin' Wolf's half-sister Mary in the 1930s. During this early period in his career he used many names such as Little Boy Blue, Willie Williamson and Willy Mither.

He began broadcasting at KFFA Radio on the legendary *King Biscuit Time* show in 1941 where he was known as Sonny Boy Williamson, taking the name from his hero, John Lee "Sonny Boy" Williamson. The radio show made him famous.

In the early 1950s he recorded on the Trumpet label in Jackson, Mississippi, along with Elmore James. Owing to his increasing popularity, he began working the bars of Detroit and Chicago. He joined Chess Records in 1955 and in 1963 began to tour Europe at the behest of Willie Dixon. Williamson's strange appearance as well as his music made him extremely memorable to his audiences. He would wear a jester's suit, bowler hat and a goatee beard and he weaved back and forth, snapping his fingers and clicking his tongue. On the harmonica he utilised many tricks of showmanship and he even played two at once. He enjoyed touring Europe, playing his way around the new blues club circuit, and even played in Poland.

He recorded on the Storyville label in Denmark and with the jazz player Chris Barber in England. He also recorded with the British blues bands the Animals and the Yardbirds. On returning to the States he rejoined the *King Biscuit Time* show.

He died quietly in his sleep in 1965.

Above: Sonny Boy Williamson – the Blues Troubadour.

BIOGRAPHY:

John Lee Hooker

John Lee Hooker was born August 1917 near Clarksdale, Mississippi. His first musical experiences were in the playing and singing of spirituals. He began to learn the guitar in 1928 but it was not until his stepfather, Will Moore, truly inspired him that he began to take it more seriously. Moore had played with Charley Patton and Son House amongst others.

In 1933 he left Mississippi and moved to Memphis and began working at a local cinema. During this time he worked with Robert Nighthawk, Eddie Love and Joe Willard. He moved to Cincinnati in 1935 and began working with blues and gospel groups such as the Delta Big Four and the Fairfield Four in the evenings. The story goes that T-Bone Walker gave John Lee Hooker his first electric guitar in 1947.

In 1943 he moved to Detroit, Michigan. Hooker's first recording "Sally May" was released, with "Boogie Chillen'" on the B-side, in November 1948 on the Modern label and it was the B-side that became his first million-selling record. Before his next record was released, at least four others were recorded by him under different pseudonyms – in fact he worked under several names, such as Poor Joe and Poor Slim, for various Detroit producers. He had follow-up success with his songs "I'm in the Mood", "Crawling Kingsnake" and "Hobo Blues". He continued to release records,

sometimes as John Lee Booker, Johnny Williams or Texas Slim. In 1951 and 1952 he recorded two sessions for Chess Records. In between these sessions he recorded his biggest hit "I'm In the Mood" for Modern Records in Detroit. He toured with his own band the Boogie Ramblers and when his contract with Modern Records finished he signed with Vee-Jay Records and began recording in Chicago.

In 1965 Hooker began recording in New York, having signed with ABC Records after Vee-Jay's bankruptcy, and in 1970 moved to California and regularly recorded in Los Angeles and San Francisco with his Coast-to-Coast Blues Band. Many famous rock musicians backed him in the 1970s. His son, Robert Hooker, toured with him during the 1980s and 1990s. He died peacefully in his sleep in June 2001.

Above: John Lee Hooker – the Boogie Man.

BIOGRAPHY:

B B King

Riley King was born September 1925 near to Indianola, Mississippi to a family of sharecroppers. When he was in his mid-teens he started busking on street corners. In 1947 he hitchhiked to Memphis and a year later got his big break by performing on Sonny Boy Williamson's radio show on KWEM. He then got a ten-minute spot on a black American radio station WDIA called King's Spot which became so popular it was changed into the Sepia Swing Club. At this time he was known as the Beale Street Blues Boy, after the famous street in Memphis in which he played the clubs, and this was soon shortened to Blues Boy King and eventually just to B B King.

In 1949 he bought a Gibson guitar and amplifier. He had played a barn dance in Arkansas at which a woman named Lucille caused a fight which resulted in a stove being knocked over and the barn was burned down. Rather than lose his precious guitar he battled through the flames and saved it. After this he would always call his guitars Lucille in memory of the incident. He is considered the man responsible for introducing sustained feedback into the blues.

King spent the 1950s on the road, following the release of his first No 1 single "Three O'Clock Blues" in 1951. Owing to the decline of the blues in the late 1950s, his popularity began to wane.

However, in 1961 King was able to sign a three-album deal with the ABC label which kept him busy during the lull. It was not until 1969 with the release of his single "The Thrill is Gone" from the groundbreaking album *Completely Well* that he gained a newer and wider audience. This popularity continues to the present day and he continues to record and win awards for his innovative sound and firm playing.

Another King of the blues was Albert King, probably one of the most under-rated bluesmen. His influence on Eric Clapton, Jeff Beck and Jimmy Page alone means that without him there would have been a huge empty space in popular music.

Above: B B King – King of the Blues.

BIOGRAPHY:

Albert King

Albert Nelson was born in April 1924 in Indianola, Mississippi, into a large family and in the 1940s moved to Arkansas. He first learned to play guitar on a homemade version, a "diddly bow", which consisted of a wire attached to a wall on which he would move a bottle to get a sound. It was not until his late teens that he was able to afford a real guitar although he only knew a few songs. By day he drove a bulldozer but played with local bands in the evenings, even playing drums at one point. It is unclear how he got the name King, but early on he would claim B B King was his brother and indeed they both had been born in the same town.

He released his first recording "Bad Luck Blues" in 1953. Unfortunately it was not a success so he went back to playing in his home town area. Although he had a hit single in 1959, it was not until the 1960s that he achieved fame for his skilful blend of blues and soul music. In 1966 he signed up to the Stax label and recorded with Booker T and the MGs. His songs "The Hunter" and "Born Under a Bad Sign" were released over the following two years on the Atlantic label and these, combined with his dedicated playing of US college circuits, ensured respect for his work. British blues bands such as Cream and Free covered these songs and King developed an underground following. In 1968 he was to release a live album *Live Wire/Blues Power* which catapulted his career into the mainstream. Also, because King's playing style was unique, in part due to playing his infamous custom flying-V called "Lucy" upside down, many artists including Eric Clapton tried to emulate his sound. King's strange tuning and razor-sharp picking skills were also legendary.

Throughout the 1970s he continued to release a mix of studio and live albums and was sought out by many of the top artists of the time. Although he suffered a five-year recording lull in the late 1970s, he returned to form in 1983 with more albums and even worked with Stevie Ray Vaughan, who idolised him. He continued to tour until his death in December 1992, when he suffered a major heart attack whilst staying in Memphis.

Above: Albert King – another King of the Blues.

THE RISE OF ROCK 'N' ROLL

In order to appeal to a wider audience, and in particular a white American audience, the blues needed to evolve. The arrival of the electric guitar and amplification represented the beginning of that evolution and, as technology improved, there was little demand for the solo artist in the mainstream, whether it be folk or blues, playing an acoustic guitar. The blues in its purest form began to decline in popularity in the USA. Also, many white American artists such as Elvis Presley used the blues format to create their own style of music which mixed blues with white American country music. By the late 1950s the blues scene in America had given way to rock 'n' roll for white audiences and soul and gospel took over for black audiences. During the early part of the next decade an unexpected phenomenon was to reverse all of this, when the blues was returned to popularity in America by British blues bands.

One of the early proponents of this crossover was the rockin' Chuck Berry who brought the wildness and exuberance of the early blues performers onto a modern stage on both sides of the Atlantic.

Above: Many white American artists such as Elvis Presley used the blues format to create their own style of music.

BIOGRAPHY:
Chuck Berry

Charles Edward Anderson Berry was born October 1926 in St Louis, Missouri into a middle-class family. He attended the first black high school west of the Mississippi, whose other alumni include Tina Turner.

His first public appearance was at his high school in the All Men's Review of 1941 singing "Confessing the Blues", a song he later recorded on 1960 album *Rockin' At the Hops*. In 1944, before he graduated, he encountered his first problem with the authorities by joyriding with two companions, for which he was arrested, charged with armed robbery and given a ten-year sentence. It was in prison that he joined a gospel choir and was released, having only served three years. In 1948 he married Themetta Suggs and worked at odd jobs including photography.

On New Year's Eve 1952 he was invited to join the Sir John's Trio and, with his great showmanship and knowledge of blues and R&B, became as popular as Ike Turner and Albert King in the St Louis area. In 1954 Berry visited Chicago and met Leonard Chess who asked him to return and record "Maybelline" with Willie Dixon on bass. Chess passed the copy on to the disc jockey Alan Freed who played it for two hours straight on his radio show. The single went on to sell over a million copies and was an overnight success. Berry continued to record but it was not until "Roll

Above: Chuck Berry – the Father of Rockin' Blues.

Over Beethoven" that he managed to achieve the same success as his first single. In March 1957 he released "School Days" which was a Top 5 hit and led to a sell-out national tour of the States. For the next two-and-a-half years he had an unbroken string of chart hits such as "Rock 'n' Roll Music", "Sweet Little Sixteen", "Johnny B Goode" and "Carol". Berry also appeared in three films, all produced by the rock 'n' roll DJ Alan Freed.

With all the money from his success he bought 30 acres of land in Wentzville, Missouri and in 1958 opened Club Bandstand in St Louis. Unfortunately, the club became the victim of racism as it was located in a white professional district and the police soon closed it down in the wake of the scandal that very nearly put an end to Berry's career. On 1 December 1959, Berry met a young native American girl called Janice Escalanti in El Paso, Texas and he arranged a job for her at his club. However, she was fired after two weeks and then she called the local police to find a way to get back home. Subsequently Berry was charged with violating the Mann Act, which covered the transportation of a minor across state lines for immoral purposes. Berry was once again sentenced to prison, this time for three years along with a US$10,000 fine.

During Berry's incarceration, many musicians began to release covers of his songs. For example, the Beach Boys released "Surfin' USA" which was a copy of "Sweet Little Sixteen". In Britain, the Rolling Stones released the Berry tune "Come On" as their first single. Five days before his release on 18 October 1963, 15 million viewers watched the Beatles, who had begun their rise to the top with covers of Berry's "Rock 'n' Roll Music" and "Roll Over Beethoven", perform on *Sunday Night at the London Palladium*. Once Berry was released, Chess Records released six of his singles, all of which made the Top 100. However, the next seven years saw a decline in his career as the rise of white urban rock 'n' roll took over the world. In a twist of irony he, as one of the greatest popular song writers, achieved his only No 1 hit with a smutty little ditty entitled "My Ding-a-Ling" which became his best-selling single ever in July 1972. In 1977 his song "Johnny B Goode" was launched into space via the *Voyager* spacecraft.

His last album was released in 1979 and he has been dogged by controversy ever since. That same year he was once more imprisoned but on tax evasion charges and his reputation for being difficult and unpredictable has prevented him from touring. In 1987 his autobiography was released, followed by a film entitled *Hail, Hail Rock 'n' Roll*. Now in his late 70s, he occasionally performs on stage and still manages to give an energetic and exciting show.

"Roll over Beethoven and dig these rhythm and blues"

(CHUCK BERRY – "ROLL OVER BEETHOVEN")

Above: Chuck Berry.

THE HISTORY OF THE BLUES GUITAR

Each era of blues music has its definitive guitars. In the 1960s Jimi Hendrix made the Fender Stratocaster the definitive rock blues instrument and in the 1970s the Gibson Les Paul defined the heavy rock blues sound. However, in the early days of blues there was no amplification and two particular guitars stand out amongst all the others; the Stella guitar and the National Resonator which was five times as loud as any guitar made of wood.

STELLA GUITARS

Stella Guitars were originally made by the Oscar Schmidt Company. The company was founded in 1879 and by the early 1900s had five factories in Europe as well as a factory in Jersey City, New Jersey in the United States. They made all kinds of stringed instruments such as mandolins, harps, banjos and guitars and also made components for other types of instruments. The guitars they produced were Sovereign, La Scala, Galiano and Stella. No two guitars were exactly the same because they were handmade in the Italian 19th-century style of craftsmanship. During the Hawaian guitar craze of the early 1920s, Koa and Tigerstripe mahogany were added to the standard birch or spruce-top range. However, the vast majority of Stellas were constructed of birch and many were made with elaborate mother-of-pearl inlaid fingerboards. They produced four body sizes: the three-quarter size, standard size, grand concert size and auditorium size, each size representing an increase in volume.

Schmidt salesmen travelled the length and breadth of the United States during the early 20s, making their instruments available in general stores. Blues musicians

Above: A Stella guitar label seen through the strings on the inside of the guitar.

living in the south, far from the city, chose to play these Stellas because they were cheap and available locally, yet they also had an element of quality. The following bluesmen are known to have used Stella guitars:

Blind Lemon Jefferson, Willie Brown, Furry Lewis, Blind Willie McTell, Charlie Lincoln, Buddy Boy Hawkins, Pegleg Howell, Blind Willie Johnson, Jim Baxter, Ed Bell, Sam Collins, Jim Jackson, Robert Nighthawk, Henry Thomas, Lulu Jackson, Lil McClintock, Leadbelly and Charley Patton.

Charley Patton is said to have preferred his Stella to a Gibson because the Stella was louder and it was volume that was important before the days of amplification.

By the late 20s the Oscar Schmidt Company had grown very large and was involved in many different aspects of the music business, including importing and manufacturing dozens of different instruments, publishing sheet music, running music schools and selling instruments door-to-door. By 1926 the company owned a number of subsidiaries including the Phonoharp Company, the International Music Corporation and Newark New Jersey which was a manufacturer's advertising company. However, when the stock market crash occurred that launched the Depression, the company, like so many others, began to fall apart. The founder Oscar Schmidt also died whilst overseas on a business trip.

The Oscar Schmidt Company continued to sell their zither and auto-harps and it was during this time that

Leadbelly's famous 12-stringed guitar was produced at the same New Jersey factory. In 1935 a man named John Carner formed the "Stella Company" and took over the production and sale of Stella guitars. In 1940, the whole business was transferred to the ownership of a company called Harmony. Harmony now manufactured their own guitars using the brand name of Stella for their low-end, flat-top guitars. Harmony continued to produce birch-bodied Stella 12-stringed guitars into the 1960s but their quality was not as high as the old Schmidt-produced Stellas.

Above: No two Stella guitars were exactly the same because they were handmade in the Italian 19th-century style of craftsmanship.

NATIONAL STEEL GUITAR

The National Steel Guitar was created by George Beauchamp and John Dopyera. Beauchamp's idea was to create a wild-looking Hawaiian guitar which sat on a stand and had a horn on the bottom and Dopyera built it, even though he knew the idea would not work in practice. Dopyera then experimented with various materials including fibreglass and tin. He settled on a very thin conical-shaped aluminium resonator design used in a set of three, connected with a t-bar inside an all-metal body. He used three cones because he found the tone was louder. He applied for a patent on this guitar in 1927 and called it the tri-cone. By 1928 the company was producing hundreds of them every week.

During the Great Depression, the company decided to produce a lower-cost guitar and came up with a single resonator which in fact saved the company from going under. Although the National was originally intended for the Hawaiian and jazz market, the fact that it was popular as a loud instrument among blues artists helped the company to survive. Dopyera then left the National and started his own company under the name Dobro Manufacturing which made single-cone resonator guitars to a new design. Later the two companies merged to become one company.

Above: A National Steel Guitar.

In 1928 Tampa Red became the first black blues artist to record with a National Steel Resonator guitar on the Vocalion label. He was followed by a large number of bluesmen such as Son House, Bukka White, Bo Carter, Blind Boy Fuller, Walter Vincent, Peetie Wheatstraw, Scrapper Blackwell, Bumblebee Slim and Black Ace.

BOTTLENECK SLIDE GUITAR

The banjo was the usual instrument for blues musicians but when guitars became more easily available, many musicians made the transition and even more just picked up the guitar first off.

In 1885, Joseph Kekuku, a student from Honolulu, began experimenting with using objects to make different musical sounds on his guitar strings. One day while walking along the railway tracks, for instance, he picked up a steel bolt; over the next few years he continued to experiment with a hair comb, a tumbler and finally a smooth steel bar made in the school shop. Until his death in 1932 he toured the USA and most of Europe teaching and popularising the Hawaiian steel guitar. The spreading popularity of the Hawaiian guitar brought it to many areas where the bluesmen were able to start experimenting with the technique. By the 1930s sliding the strings had developed into two distinct styles. One was the Hawaiian guitar style, particularly suited to National Steel Resonator guitars, and the other was the bottleneck style which became popular among blues guitarists, particularly the innovative Robert Johnson, B B King, John Lee Hooker, Duane Allman, Ry Cooder and Jimmy Page.

The easiest way to learn to play guitar was to tune to an open chord, using E or A and then bar the frets. Guitars were not as resistant to weather changes in their early days as they are today, and the necks would often bow, raising the strings up higher and farther than the fretboard. In order to compensate, players barred the strings with pocket knives, combs or spikes. Even as far back as the late 1800s people played guitars and banjos by sliding such objects up and down the strings with one hand whilst picking the strings with the other.

Above: The bottleneck style – popular among blues guitarists.

Above: Muddy Waters experimented with the instrument's tonal and harmonic possibilities and in the process inspired other musicians to take up the new electric guitar sound.

THE ELECTRIC GUITAR

The idea of using electricity to amplify stringed instruments began to be feasible during the late 1920s. Lloyd Loar experimented with electrification as early as 1923 and developed an electro-static pickup that sensed vibrations in the sound board. In 1931 George Beauchamp of National Steel Guitars, working with Adolph Rickenbacker in 1931, produced an electro-magnetic pickup which was used on a lap steel guitar. This was the first commercial electric guitar.

By the late 1930s, this new technology had been adapted to the more traditional Spanish-style hollow-body wooden guitars. However, because of their internal acoustics, there were problems with distortions, overtones and feedbacks. Guitarist and inventor Les Paul addressed these problems by mounting the strings and pickups on a solid body of pine, thereby minimising body vibrations. During the 1940s Paul Bigsby and Leo Fender also began experimenting with solid-body guitars.

During the early years of its existence, the electric guitar's viability as a real musical instrument was often debated. The instrument's detractors often claimed it did not produce a pure, "authentic" musical sound. However, early electric guitar pioneers of the 1930s and 1940s, particularly the blues masters T-Bone Walker and Muddy Waters, experimented with the instrument's tonal and harmonic possibilities and in the process inspired other musicians to take up the new electric guitar sound. Many traditional bluesmen, however, shunned this new innovation and it was not until the 1950s when rock 'n' roll became the sound of the day that the electric guitar came into its own. The electric guitar was at the heart of the cultural revolution that rock 'n' roll symbolised. Rock 'n' roll was really an electrified expression of traditional 12-bar blues.

Above: The electric guitar was at the heart of the cultural revolution that rock n' roll symbolised.

Rock n' roll was really an electrified expression of traditional 12-bar blues

BLUES REVIVALISTS 1960-2003

"There's just certain styles of playing that you do play in your own way. Maybe it's in the way your fingers bend, for all I know. And so whenever you pick up the guitar it's not so much the sound of the instrument itself, it's like the thing that you add onto it – the attitude."

(KEITH RICHARDS)

BRITISH BLUES

During World War II, American GIs brought many records of American music with them to Britain. The British public became huge fans of this upbeat music that was coming across the Atlantic, raising their spirits even in the face of German bombing raids. After the war and during the early 1950s American blues artists had been brought to England by Chris Barber who was the leader of a jazz band that included a small group dedicated to American blues. Big Bill Broonzy was the first American bluesman of any note to appear in England and Europe and he made the first of his many recordings for France's Vogue label on that first visit. Ironically, Broonzy did not play the material he was

most closely associated with in America. He was, at that time, one of Chicago's top bluesmen but the British were looking for something much purer. So Broonzy adopted a deliberately archaic country blues style and played songs that he had never played for the American market. His acoustic sets included folk songs as well as country blues and protest material. When he returned in 1955, he recorded for Pye Records.

In 1958 Muddy Waters visited England and single-handedly inspired a whole generation of young white urban males to go out, buy guitars and become electric blues musicians. When Muddy first went on stage in England he was backed by Otis Spann and some members of Chris Barber's jazz band and he played an electric, solid-body Fender guitar. This was a great shock to British audiences who associated the blues with acoustic music. However, the hip young men about town saw this innovation and immediately set about copying his electric style and increasing the decibel rate through larger and larger amplifiers. After the initial shock of seeing Muddy Waters playing electric blues, the music press covered his shows with unbridled enthusiasm and his concerts attracted thousands of fans from all over the British Isles.

THE MARQUEE CLUB

Also in 1958 Chris Barber, who had been bringing over the American bluesmen, formed a partnership with Harold Pendleton and opened a jazz club in Oxford Street called the Marquee Club. At the beginning of the 1960s the Marquee was the premier British blues venue. Pendleton began to bring in black American blues musicians who were very quickly emulated by the London lads. The club soon became a steamy, stomping rave of a nightclub. In 1962, Blues Incorporated were given a residency at the Marquee and recorded their first album – the first blues album ever made in England. In 1964, the Marquee moved from its basement in Oxford Street to a disused warehouse in Wardour Street, Soho. The Soho club was an odd shape with a long corridor, leading to an oblong room. Pendleton brought with him the striped awning that had covered the stage at the Oxford Street club and that gave the club its name. During that year the Marquee became the UK's prime rhythm and blues venue, with all the top bands playing, from the Rolling Stones, the Yardbirds and Manfred Mann through to Cream, Jeff Beck and the Faces. During the next three decades the Marquee dominated the music scene and became the ultimate platform for even the most established of acts. It became a place of myth; a club that all fledgling bands had to play in. It was almost like a music school in itself, a place to meet other musicians, and was full of glamorous women. The bands not only played there, they partied there as well. The Wardour Street Marquee closed its doors in 1988 and was mourned by the music world.

Above: Jimi Hendrix at the Marquee Club, London.

BRITISH BLUES FESTIVALS

Prior to the Marquee's success, Barber and Pendleton had been promoting jazz and had set up the National Jazz and Blues Festival which eventually became the longest-running of the UK rock festivals. It is still running to this day, albeit under a different title and with completely different music to that period, but nevertheless the continuity in attitude is there. The Reading Festival, as it is now known, has barely a hint of jazz and its blues content is limited to heavy rock riffs but the atmosphere remains the same.

When Barber and Pendleton began the first National Jazz Festival in 1961 they must have had little idea that it would mutate into a melting pot of electric blues, pop, folk and rock. The first festivals featured the likes of jazz stalwarts Chris Barber, Johnny Dankworth and the Clyde Valley Stompers but the new generation of teenagers was discovering rhythm and blues and each year more of these artists were added to the bill. There was Georgie Fame and Long John Baldry, and in 1963 the relatively unknown Rolling Stones appeared, being paid the meagre sum of £30. By the following year the Stones were top of the bill and taking 50 per cent of the night's takings. There were many overseas artists playing such as Memphis Slim and Jimmy Witherspoon, alongside, over the years, British acts such the Yardbirds, the Who, Cream, Spencer Davis, Traffic, the Small Faces, Jethro Tull, the Nice, Family, Fleetwood Mac, John Mayall, Blodwyn Pig, Pink Floyd,

Incredible String Band, Fairport Convention, Crazy World of Arthur Brown, Tyrannosaurus Rex, Bonzo Dog Doo Dah Band, Colosseum and Joe Cocker all played. No wonder the name of the festival was changed to the National Jazz and Blues Festival.

In 1965 the festival was held in Richmond for the last time. The locals objected to the increased number of fans sleeping out rough in Richmond Park, and the increase in decibels from the PA systems further aggravated the situation. In 1966 the festival shifted to Windsor and included the following among its line-up: Georgie Fame, Spencer Davis, Chris Farlowe, the Move and the Small Faces.

1967 was the last year that Windsor would be used but by this time the festival included many unheard-of luxury facilities such as toilets, a camping ground and medical stations. The line-up included: the Small Faces, the Nice, the Move, Paul Jones, Crazy World of Arthur Brown, Zoot Money's Big Roll Band, Aynsley Dunbar's Retaliation, Ten Years After, Cream, Jeff Beck, John Mayall's Bluesbreakers, Chicken Shack, Fleetwood Mac and Pentangle amongst others.

The National Jazz and Blues Festival continued throughout the 1960s and 1970s, the emphasis slowly moving away to pop and rock.

In 1969 festival promoter Freddie Bannister launched the Bath Blues Festival, featuring the cream of British

blues bands and a few progressive rock groups. The line-up included Led Zeppelin, John Mayall, Fleetwood Mac, Ten Years After, Colosseum, Blodwyn Pig, Keef Hartley, Taste, Roy Harper, Savoy Brown Blues Band, Champion Jack Dupree, the Nice and the Liverpool Scene. The festival, held in the centre of Bath, was attended by around 30,000 people. The following year the Bath festival moved to nearby Shepton Mallet showground and the line-up included the greatest rock bands that the world had ever seen playing together. It was at this point that electric blues separated from progressive rock and the only real blues band to play

at the 1970 Bath Festival of Blues were the headliners Led Zeppelin.

The blues festival scene continues to this day with small festivals being promoted. Audiences of 5,000 to 10,000 still camp out for the weekend throughout the UK, Europe and the USA. But the days of the monster festivals have long gone.

One of the most influential and inspirational people on the British music scene was Alexis Korner.

Above: Led Zeppelin at the 1970 Bath Blues Festival.

BIOGRAPHY:

Alexis Korner

Alexis Korner was born in April 1928 in Paris, France. In 1958 he met Cyril Davies at the London Skiffle Club where they were both playing in skiffle bands. Both of them were frustrated by the limitations of the genre and decided to transform the venue into the London Blues and Barrelhouse Club. This club became famous for showcasing visiting American black bluesmen.

The jazz trombonist Chris Barber had also decided to move into the rhythm and blues genre and began by employing Korner on guitar and Davies on harmonica to back the blues singer Ottilie Patterson. In 1961, Alexis Korner formed Blues Incorporated and the following year opened up the Ealing Rhythm and Blues Club in a West London basement. Blues Incorporated had Charlie Watts on drums, Art Wood on vocals and Keith Scott on piano as well as Korner and Davies. Over the following years other aspiring musicians moved in and out of Blues Incorporated, as if it was a blues school. These musicians included Long John Baldry, Jack Bruce (Cream), Graham Bond (Graham Bond Organisation), Ginger Baker (Cream), Mick Jagger (Rolling Stones) and Paul Jones (Manfred Mann), all of whom went on to have very successful careers in the British music industry.

In the early days Blues Incorporated went largely unnoticed by the general public and the name was dropped in 1966. Korner formed Free At Last in 1967, New Church in 1969, CCS in 1970 and Snape in 1972. CCS recorded "Whole Lotta Love" in 1970 which was used as a signature tune for *Top of the Pops* and Korner also had a BBC Radio 1 show and a long-running show for the BBC World Service.

For his 50th birthday party, he joined Charlie Watts, Ian Stewart, Jack Bruce, Dick Heckstall-Smith, Eric Clapton, Chris Farlowe and Zoot Money on stage and this was recorded and filmed. In 1981, Korner began an ambitious television documentary on the history of rock. Sadly his health began to deteriorate. In January 1984 he died of cancer and left the documentary and a number of other projects uncompleted. His influence on the British blues and rock scene is incalculable.

The other "school" for blues and rock musicians was run by John Mayall.

Above: Alexis Korner.

BIOGRAPHY:

John Mayall

John Mayall was born in November 1933 in Macclesfield, Cheshire. His father had an extensive jazz record collection which was to influence John from a very early age. By the age of 13, Mayall was playing guitar, piano and harmonica in the style of Leadbelly.

During his 20s he trained at art school, spent three years of National Service in the British Army based in Korea and had a successful career in graphic design. From 1956 until 1962, Mayall began to perform publicly, fronting the Powerhouse Four and later Blues Incorporated. It was not until the age of 30 that his career as a professional bluesman began.

At the beginning of the British blues boom in the 1960s, Alexis Korner encouraged Mayall to move to London where he was able to turn fully professional with his band John Mayall's Bluesbreakers. A couple of years later he met his soulmate in Eric Clapton, a union that culminated in the Bluesbreakers' first hit album *Bluesbreakers* and brought them worldwide legendary status. When Clapton and Jack Bruce left the Bluesbreakers to form Cream they were succeeded by a series of great musicians such as Peter Green, John McVie and Mick Fleetwood who all went into Fleetwood Mac; Andy Fraser who formed Free; and Mick Taylor who joined the Rolling Stones, following the death of Brian Jones.

Mayall moved to the USA in 1970 to capitalise on his popularity there. He moved to Laurel Canyon in Los Angeles, and began forming bands composed of American musicians such as Blue Mitchell, Red Holloway, Larry Taylor and Harvey Mandel. Mayall also backed John Lee Hooker, T-Bone Walker and Sonny Boy Williamson on their first British tour.

In 1979, with his career at an all-time low, fire destroyed his Laurel Canyon home, taking with it his diaries, his master recordings, extensive book and magazine collections and his own designs and artwork. In 1982, joined by Mick Taylor and John McVie, he reformed the Bluesbreakers for a couple of tours and a film entitled *Blues Alive*, which featured Albert King, Buddy Guy, Junior Wells and Etta James amongst others. In 1984 guitarists Coco Montoya and Walter Trout joined the Bluesbreakers, followed by Joe Yuele on drums.

Mayall has continued to release blues/jazz/rock fusion albums over the decades. In 2001, came *Along for the Ride* featuring an all-star line-up, many of whom had apprenticed with him in the Bluesbreakers. These included Mick Taylor, Mick Fleetwood, John McVie, Billy Gibbons, Jonny Lang, Steve Miller, Billy Preston, Otis Rush, Gary Moore, Jeff Healey and many more. This was the first time that the original Fleetwood Mac members had appeared together for over 30 years.

Above: John Mayall.

In August 2002, the album *Stories* was released, going straight to No 1 in the US album charts. John Mayall is now in his 70s, the father of six children, has six grandchildren and shows no signs of slowing down in both his touring and recording projects.

Above: John Mayall shows no sign of slowing down.

Fleetwood Mac began life as a hard-edged British blues band in the late 1960s and evolved into one of the most polished pop-rock acts in the world. Throughout all their changes, Mick Fleetwood on drums and John McVie on bass have remained at the core.

BIOGRAPHY:

Fleetwood Mac

The roots of Fleetwood Mac lie in John Mayall's legendary Bluesbreakers. John McVie joined the Bluesbreakers in 1963, and in 1966 Peter Green replaced Eric Clapton. A year later Mick Fleetwood joined on drums. Inspired by the success of other blues bands the three of them broke away from Mayall and debuted at the National Jazz and Blues Festival in August 1967. Jeremy Spencer joined to play slide guitar with the band. They signed with Blue Horizon and released their first album *Fleetwood Mac* in 1968.

During 1968 the band also added guitarist Danny Kirwan and the following year they recorded *Fleetwood Mac In Chicago*, with Willie Dixon and Otis Spann in the line-up. In 1969 they released two albums – *English Rose* and *Play On* which showed that the band were moving away from their blues roots. That year Peter Green's "Man of the World" and "Oh Well" both reached the top of the UK charts. Green suddenly

left the band in the spring of 1970 and released two solo albums during the 70s but was scarcely heard of again until the late-1990s. He was replaced with Christine Perfect, a vocalist and pianist who had been working with Chicken Shack and Spencer Davis. In 1971 she married John McVie and changed her surname accordingly.

Above: Fleetwood Mac – platinum blues.

The next album, *Kiln House*, was dominated by Jeremy Spencer but, like Peter Green, he too had ongoing mental problems due to heavy drug use. During the band's 1971 American tour Spencer disappeared and it was later discovered that he had joined the religious cult the Children of God. Christine McVie's and Danny Kirwan's influence moved the band towards mainstream rock but on the next album *Bare Trees* in 1972 new guitarist Bob Welch exerted a heavy influence on their sound. In 1972 guitarist Kirwan was fired and replaced by Bob Weston and Dave Walker. They both appeared on the 1973 album *Penguin* but left soon thereafter. In 1974 the group's manager Clifford Davis formed a fake Fleetwood Mac, trying to cash in on their huge popularity, that toured the USA. The real Mac won a lawsuit against him.

In 1974 Fleetwood Mac moved to California and recruited Americans Lindsey Buckingham and Stevie Nicks; the band changed direction again to a blues/pop/rock fusion. Their first album with the new line-up sold over five million copies in the USA alone and the follow-up album *Rumours* sold over 17 million copies stateside, making it the second-biggest-selling album of all time. They continued to release albums all through the 1980s. In 1991 the band released the boxed set *25 Years*.

Band members now guest with various artists or have successful solo careers. As a band they have a new album out in 2003 and plan to do a world tour as well.

Above; Fleetwood Mac.

ELECTRIC BLUES

"Pagey plays from somewhere else. I like to think of it as ... a little left of heaven"

(ROBERT PLANT – LED ZEPPELIN)

BIOGRAPHY:

Jeff Beck

From the 1960s onwards a new phenomenon could be seen; the guitar hero. Although all these musicians have crossed many musical boundaries into rock, folk and world it is the influence of the blues that can be heard the most while they strut their stuff on stage.

Jeffrey Beck was born in June 1944 in Wallington, Surrey. His first musical interest was as a choirboy, but by the age of 11 he had started to learn to play guitar. After attending Wimbledon Art School in London, he joined the infamous Screaming Lord Sutch band and in 1965, following the departure of Eric Clapton, was invited to join the Yardbirds. Whilst with the group he took the group's sound into the realm of psychedelia. At the end of 1966 he left the Yardbirds and enlisted Rod Stewart on vocals, Ron Wood on bass, Nicky Hopkins on keyboards and Aynsley Dunbar on drums for his Jeff Beck Group. They released the metallic blues album *Truth* in 1968 and the following year released *Beckola*.

The following year Rod and Ron left to join the Faces. Beck enlisted Bobby Tench on vocals and Clive Chaman on bass, Max Middleton on keyboards and Cozy Powell on drums, releasing *Rough and Ready* in 1972. In 1973, Beck formed a power trio with former Vanilla Fudge members Carmine Appice on drums and Tim Bogert on bass. In 1975 George Martin produced Beck's album *Blow by Blow* and in 1976 he released *Wired*, working with Jan Hammer on keyboards.

He collaborated with Hammer again in 1980 on the album *There and Beck*.

After a five-year break from music, he returned in 1985 with a pop/rock album *Flash* which featured the single "People Get Ready" sung by former band member Rod Stewart.

Beck's main interest outside music is car restoration and since the 1980s he has regularly taken breaks from music, making only the odd guest appearance with artists such as Tina Turner, Mick Jagger, Roger Waters, Robert Plant and Jimmy Page and also a short tour with Stevie Ray Vaughan.

In 1993 he recorded a tribute album to Gene Vincent called *Crazy Legs* and in March 1999 released his first album of original material for more than a decade. He also played on the Yardbirds' album of 2003, *Birdland*.

He continues to inspire many young musicians with his innovative and stylish guitar work.

Above: Jeff Beck – blues deluxe.

BIOGRAPHY:

Eric Clapton

Eric Patrick Fryer was born in March 1945 in Ripley, Surrey. He was raised by his grandparents Rose and Jack Clapp and they were responsible for giving him his first guitar. As a child, his main musical inspiration was Jerry Lee Lewis. He went to Kingston College of Art to study glass design but was expelled for being inattentive in class (he kept playing guitar). He joined a number of British blues bands including the Roosters and Casey Jones and the Engineers and then in 1963 joined the Yardbirds who became a sensation for their blues/rock fusion.

Clapton earned the name "Slowhand" because his string-bending style often resulted in broken guitar strings which he would replace in the middle of a song, accompanied by a slow hand clap from the audience. Because the Yardbirds began to move more towards pop singles and away from pure blues, he left in 1965 and joined John Mayall's Bluesbreakers which is where he earned his other nickname "God". In 1966 he left the Bluesbreakers and formed the volatile supergroup Cream with bassist Jack Bruce and drummer Ginger Baker. In 1969, following the departure of Bruce, the band mutated into Blind Faith, with Stevie Winwood on vocals/keyboards and Rick Grech on bass; they recorded one incredible album together. Blind Faith disbanded in less than a year after a very successful US tour. Clapton then went on to tour with Delaney & Bonnie and played on one live album with them before releasing his first solo album in 1970. *Eric Clapton* was disappointingly received apart from the pop hit "After Midnight". The musicians who had played on it, however, were retained and Clapton recruited Duane Allman; together they formed Derek and the Dominos, releasing the classic album *Layla and Other Assorted Love Songs*. The line-up crumbled on their American tour due to Clapton's increasing dependence on hard drugs. He underwent a successful rehabilitation treatment following the advice of the Who's Pete Townshend and returned with a role in the rock opera *Tommy*.

His post-rehabilitation style was far more laid-back and he began to sing and enjoy himself more on his albums. Unfortunately, he moved from drug addiction to alcoholism but was still able to release a string of successful albums in the 1980s. In 1988 Polygram released a retrospective four-CD set featuring all of his best works called *Crossroads*. This received a Grammy Award.

In 1990 three of his best friends were killed in a helicopter crash, including Stevie Ray Vaughan, and a few months later his son Conor fell out of an apartment window to his death. In 1992, having channelled his grief into his music, Clapton wrote the

song "Tears in Heaven" and in that same year received a total of six Grammies as well as releasing a live album *Unplugged*.

In 1994 Clapton returned to the field of traditional blues with the release of the critically acclaimed album *From the Cradle*. Three years later, in 1997, he picked up further awards for *Change The World*. In 2001 he released *One More Car, One More Tour*, which was his first live album since 1992. He has continued to astonish and delight a wide spectrum of music lovers from all walks of life.

Above: Eric Clapton.

BIOGRAPHY:

Jimmy Page

James Patrick Page was born in Heston, Middlesex, in 1944. He grew up heavily influenced by American blues artists and first learned to play acoustic guitar at the age of 13. Although he had started art college it was during his teens that he began work as a session guitarist and it was not long before he gave up college. He was playing Chicago blues at the Marquee Club when he was first discovered. In 1965 he was invited to join the Yardbirds but initially turned it down as he believed that his session work paid more. However, he was later persuaded and together with Keith Relf on vocals, Chris Dreja on bass and Jim McCarty on drums achieved great artistic, if not commercial, success.

In 1968 the Yardbirds split and Page formed the New Yardbirds, which was to change its name to Led Zeppelin, with Robert Plant on vocals, John Paul Jones on bass and keyboards and John "Bonzo" Bonham on drums. After selling millions of albums worldwide Page was widely acknowledged as being one of the most talented guitarists in rock history. His on-stage showmanship was unprecedented as he played on his double-neck guitar with a violin bow, all the while dressed in rich velvet. The film *The Song Remains The Same* shows the band on an American tour and gives an insight into their occult leanings and the sheer presence they had on stage. In addition to playing guitar on Led Zeppelin's albums, Page also produced them.

Page had an abiding interest in the occult, particularly in the works of Aleister Crowley, and in addition to obtaining Crowley's former house Boleskine on the shores of Loch Ness, he also opened the Equinox bookshop in London which specialised in first editions of Crowley. Again, this promoted the idea of the blues as the Devil's music.

In 1980, following the death of irreplaceable drummer John Bonham, the band decided to split. In 1985 and 1986 Page released two Top 30 albums with a new quartet called the Firm and in 1988 came his solo debut album *Outrider* which featured guest appearances by Robert Plant and Jason Bonham, the son of Bonzo, on drums. In 1993, Page worked with former Whitesnake vocalist David Coverdale and in 1994 he reunited with Robert Plant for an MTV *Unplugged* special. He joined forces with Plant again in 1998 for *Walking into Clarksdale* then in 1999 joined US blues rock band the Black Crowes for a British and American tour, as well as playing on the internet album *Live at the Greek*.

Page continues to this day to play, making guest appearances with various artists, both live and in the recording studio. He has also moved into the cyber music realm and has a substantial internet presence.

Above; Jimmy Page, Led Zeppelin.

BIOGRAPHY:
Keith Richards

Keith Richards was born in December 1943 in Dartford, Kent. He was a choirboy at St Paul's Cathedral and sang in front of the Queen. He started on guitar in his early teens but it was not until he attended art school in his mid-teens that he began to take a more serious interest in the instrument. With childhood friend Mick Jagger he helped found the Rolling Stones in 1962 driven by their shared love of black American blues. They began by playing gigs around London, doing covers of Muddy Waters, Willie Dixon, Chuck Berry and others of their blues heroes. Then they began to write their own songs together.

The Rolling Stones conquered America with the classic riffing of "I Can't Get No Satisfaction". The band were the complete antithesis of the happy, shiny Beatles image. Instead, this was a group that terrified the parents of teenage girls and boys alike. The Stones were shrouded in an aura of sex, drugs and mystery. Jagger and Richards were the bad boys of rock and roll and echoes of the blues featured prominently in Richards' guitar work.

Richards was always at the forefront of controversy, beginning with his 1967 arrest on trumped-up drug charges. Over the next decade he was arrested ten times, narrowly escaping a prison sentence, and the output of the Rolling Stones suffered as a result of this. Fortunately, Richards managed to make it into the 1980s and beyond, and has since continued to work with the Rolling Stones. In 1986 he worked with one of his blues heroes – Chuck Berry. Shortly after this he released his first solo album *Talk is Cheap* with his band the Xpensive Winos. He continues to live the life of a wandering minstrel on his world tours with the Rolling Stones, much like his blues predecessors.

Above: Keith Richards, the Rolling Stones.

Above: Keith Richards.

"The night I was born,
Lord the moon stood a fire red,

Said the night I was born,
the moon turned a fire red,

My poor mother, her cryin' she said
'The gypsy was right'

And she fell right dead

I'm a voodoo chile,
Lord I'm a voodoo chile"

(VOODOO CHILE – JIMI HENDRIX)

BIOGRAPHY:
Jimi Hendrix

Johnny Allen Hendrix was born in November 1942 in Seattle, Washington. His father subsequently changed his name to James Marshall Hendrix. In his youth he spent hours listening to the blues of Robert Johnson and B B King and taught himself to play guitar. Interestingly he was left-handed but played a right-handed guitar with the strings upside down. He joined several local rhythm and blues bands whilst still at school. On leaving in 1959 he joined the US Army and during his stint as a paratrooper in the 101st Airborne Division he met Billy Cox, a bass player, who was to collaborate with him many times during his musical career. They formed the King Casuals as a US Army rock band. Hendrix was discharged in 1962 and went to work with touring revues, backing Sam Cooke, as well as the Isley Brothers, Little Richard and King Curtis, acting as session guitarist on their recordings.

In 1964 Hendrix moved to New York. Two years later he was known as Jimi James and formed a band called Jimi James and the Blueflames which included guitarist Randy California. Whilst working for a blues/ rock band he played a gig in Greenwich Village and was seen by Chas Chandler, bassist with the Animals, who persuaded Hendrix to go to London. Hendrix arrived in England in September 1966 to be managed by Chandler and, after auditioning, took on Noel Redding on bass and Mitch Mitchell on drums. The

new group called the Jimi Hendrix Experience played a string of club dates in London and recorded the album *Are You Experienced?* They then released their first single "Hey Joe" which immediately went into the UK Top Ten. This was followed up by the infamously psychedelic, "Purple Haze".

What made Hendrix stand out from other blues players of the time was the volume that he squeezed out of his Marshall amplifier, his wild and visual guitar playing, not to mention the striking clothes with which he adorned his incredibly tall figure. He used a wealth of electronic devices and played with distortion and feedback. Following in the tradition of some of the earlier bluesmen, he played his guitar behind his back or between his legs and simulated sexual ecstasy with it. After releasing his debut album, he returned to America in 1967 to play at the Monterey Pop Festival which saw him playing the guitar with his teeth and famously setting light to it with lighter fuel.

Above: Jimi Hendrix.

His next album *Axis: Bold as Love* revealed his talent as a lyricist as well as a performer. In January 1968, Hendrix embarked on a gruelling American tour, playing 54 concerts in 47 days. *Electric Ladyland*, the last official Jimi Hendrix Experience album, was released later that year. This double album was originally dismissed as self-indulgent by the critics but is now recognised as a major work of art. Unfortunately, Noel Redding was becoming increasingly frustrated with the set bass patterns he was expected to play – as well as the fact that the group's commercial success didn't seem to be reflected in their finances. The Experience played its final concert on 29 June 1969 and Redding left.

In August 1969, Hendrix's new line-up of Mitchell, Cox, Larry Lee on rhythm guitar, plus Juma Sultan and Jerry Velez both on percussion, performed as "Gypsies, Suns and Rainbows" and closed the Woodstock Festival, during which Hendrix performed his evocative rendition of "The Star Spangled Banner". The group was disbanded after Woodstock and in October Hendrix formed the all-black trio Band of Gypsys with Cox and Buddy Miles on drums. After only one album and three live concerts the band broke up. Hendrix then concentrated on work to build his Electric Ladyland recording studio and another double album *First Rays of the New Morning Sun*. This only saw the light of day when it was reconstructed in 1997. Hendrix resumed touring with Cox and Mitchell, making his final UK appearance at the Isle of Wight Festival in 1969.

Following a short European tour, he returned to London and on 18 September 1970 was found dead by his girlfriend. There have been posthumous releases and the track "Voodoo Chile" became a posthumous No 1 single.

In 1993 a tribute album, *Stone Free,* was released, which included the Pretenders, Eric Clapton, Jeff Beck and the classically trained violinist Nigel Kennedy. Hendrix is considered to be the most inventive guitarist of all time and his influence on music to this day is formidable

"Knowledge speaks but wisdom listens"

(JIMI HENDRIX)

There's a saying that "white men can't play the blues". But time and again it has been proven that the blues is something from deep within, and it is Johnny Winter above all who stands as proof of this with his spirited playing and his elfin albino appearance.

Above: Jimi Hendrix – psychedelic voodoo blues.

BIOGRAPHY:

Johnny Winter

John Dawson Winter III was born in February 1944 in Beaumont, Texas. He first learned to play at the age of five when he had lessons on the clarinet. Before long he had progressed to the guitar. At the age of14 he and his keyboard-playing younger brother Edgar formed Johnny and the Jammers in their hometown of Beaumont. They soon landed a recording contract on the Dart label. Their first single was called "Schoolboy Blues".

During the 1960s Winter worked as a session musician in Texas, as well as playing gigs with touring blues artists like B B King. In 1968 he formed a trio with Tommy Shannon on bass and Uncle John Turner on drums. Although they were drawing good crowds, their hard blues was too much for the American record companies at the time. Winter was discouraged by this lack of interest and decided to move to England. But when he returned to the USA to pick up the band, he discovered that an article had appeared in *Rolling Stone* magazine and every major record label started to call him. He signed to Columbia in one of the first million-dollar deals and the press jumped on the bandwagon, backing him to win back the crown of guitar king from Britain's dynamic guitar trio of Clapton, Page and Beck with his 1969 album *Progressive Blues Experiment*. Winter recorded four albums for Columbia and then in 1974 moved to Blue Sky where he released his

John Dawson Winter III album. He released three further solo albums and also worked as the producer on four Muddy Waters albums, two of which won him Grammy awards.

After a four-year break in recording, Winter joined Alligator Records in 1984, releasing *Guitar Slinger*, followed up with *Serious Business* and then *Third Degree* in 1986. In the 1990s he released a number of albums for which he returned to his blues roots. He has kept firmly in the blues tradition since then and, even though he has had major surgery, he still tours in the USA.

Above: Johnny Winter – illustrated bluesman.

Above: Johnny Winter.

Stevie Ray Vaughan

Stephen Ray Vaughan was born in October 1954 in Dallas, Texas. He was the younger brother to James Vaughan and both boys were given guitars in 1963. At the age of 11 Stevie Ray first started to impress people with his guitar-playing skills, particularly whilst playing a Jeff Beck song called "Jeff's Boogie". Sadly by 1965 both brothers had started to let drink and drugs into their lives and when Jimmie Vaughan moved out, the boys' parents decided to seriously curtail their younger son's music activities, believing them to be responsible for the lack of discipline in his life.

In 1970, Stevie was working as a dishwasher in a fast-food establishment when he accidentally fell into a vat of grease. This was to be a turning point in his life as it was when he decided to form the band Blackbird and dedicate his life to music. In 1971, he followed his brother Jimmie and friend Doyle Bramhall to Austin, taking Blackbird with him. It was in Austin that he began to hone his playing on the club scene there, and there that he found his favourite guitar, a 1959 Stratocaster known as "Number One".

In 1977, having almost made it to the big time on several occasions, he formed the blues band Triple Threat revue with big brother Jimmie in the line-up

After several personnel changes the band became Triple Threat and played a number of blues festivals around the United States. It was not until 1980, however, that his most famous band Double Trouble was given its name. Around this time Jimmie, too, started to attract attention with his blues band, the Fabulous Thunderbirds.

In 1981, Mick Jagger of the Rolling Stones heard a live recording of the Double Trouble playing at a blues festival in Austin. He invited them to New York to play at a Rolling Stones party. They were also invited to perform at the Montreux Jazz Festival in Switzerland, making history as the first unsigned band to do so, and there they were heard by both David Bowie and Jackson Browne. The former asked Stevie Ray to play on his *Let's Dance* album, while the latter granted the group free time in his Los Angeles recording studio, where they lay down the tracks for their first album. Stevie Ray Vaughan and Double Trouble were signed up and in 1983 released *Texas Flood*, which won two Grammy awards including Best Traditional Blues Album of the year. The following year Vaughan became the first white American to win the W C Handy National Blues Award for Entertainer of 1984 and Blues Instrumentalist of the Year. He also received nominations and awards for every one of his subsequent albums.

In 1986 years of drug and alcohol abuse started to
catch up with Vaughan and he collapsed on stage whilst
on a German tour. He attended a rehabilitation unit on
his return to Texas. Fortunately, this set him back on
track; for the next few years he made numerous guest
appearances and in 1989 Double Trouble released their
fifth album. In 1990 the *Family Style* album saw him
paired up with his older brother. This was followed up
by a two-month tour with Joe Cocker.

Vaughan performed with Buddy Guy, Eric Clapton and
Robert Cray in Wisconsin on 27 August 1990. Later
that day he left in a helicopter; tragically it crashed
into a hill during a rainstorm, and Vaughan and other
members of Clapton's entourage were killed.

*"I've said that playing the blues is like
having to be black twice. Stevie missed on
both counts but I never noticed."*

(B B KING)

Whilst there have been many female blues vocalists,
Bonnie Raitt is unusual because she also plays blues
guitar and was taught by some of the master bluesmen.

Above: Stevie Ray Vaughan.

Above: Bonnie Raitt.

BIOGRAPHY:

Bonnie Raitt

Bonnie Raitt was born in 1949, the daughter of the Broadway star John Raitt. She began learning to play Stella guitar at the age of eight. At the age of 20 she dropped out of college and began playing on the American folk and blues circuit. She quickly made a name for herself, unique in that she was a white female playing credible bottleneck guitar. Raitt worked during this time with many of the blues legends such as Howlin' Wolf and Mississippi Fred McDowell. She also recorded with the blues singer Sippie Wallace.

Raitt signed a recording contract in 1971 and her first album included songs by Stephen Stills, a number of blues covers and two self-penned songs.

The following year she released her *Give It Up* album which made the charts. She continued to release albums through the 70s and 80s and with her tenth album *Nick of Time* she finally received the commercial rewards that her body of work in the blues genre deserved. She won Grammy awards and in 1990 her work on John Lee Hooker's *The Healer* album brought her another. Over the last decade or so she has worked with numerous artists, contributed to soundtracks and furthered the cause of the blues, releasing her 16th album *Silver Lining* in 2002. She continues to tour the UK, USA and Europe, bringing her unique brand of personality, playing and political activism with her.

BIOGRAPHY:

Taj Mahal

Henry Saint Claire Fredericks was born in May 1940 in New York. His father was a West Indian jazz musician and his mother a music teacher who sang in a gospel choir. He attended the University of Massachusetts to study for a BA in Agriculture and while there developed an abiding interest in blues music, particularly that of Howlin' Wolf, Son House and Chuck Berry. He began performing in Boston folk clubs with his band the Elektras and then shortly after graduating in 1965 moved to the west coast. There he met up with Ry Cooder and Ed Cassidy and formed a band called the Rising Sons. However, when their first album was shelved he decided to continue as a solo artist although Cooder still played on his first album, simply called *Taj Mahal*, released in 1968. The album was a personal compendium of electric country blues. His second album was *The Natch'l Blues* and the third was a double album called *Giant Step/De Ole Folks at Home*, one disc of which was a traditional acoustic record whilst the other was a vibrant rock/blues album. This led to him being sought out by musicians such as B B King and Jimi Hendrix.

He has continued to record and over the years has experimented with African/American roots music as well as exploring his West Indian background. Taj Mahal has also worked on soundtracks for films and television as well as children's music. During the 1990s his music moved closer to soul and R&B. He tours regularly with an ever-evolving line-up of musicians called the International Rhythm Band and involves himself with blues education whenever he can. Indeed, he is working with the director Martin Scorsese on a television series about the blues.

Above: Taj Mahal.

EPILOGUE

Since the arrival of the World Wide Web, a whole new audience of blues aficionados has been created. Simply type the word "blues" into any of the major search engines and hundreds of relevant sites will appear. Thankfully many rare collections of blues records are available to listen to, particularly on the internet blues radio stations. The blues has come a long way from its origins in the villages of West Africa to the superhighway of the 21st century.

Today, more than ever, the blues is everywhere. Without it there would be no modern music; no rock, no rap, no country, no jazz. It is essentially simple folk music that has over time gained an urban sophistication. It is blue, it is black, it is white, it is every colour. It is sadness personified, yet it can uplift your spirits and make you want to dance. Long live the blues and those who play it.

INDEX